Penguin Education

Penguin Modern Psychology
General Editor B. M. Foss

Social Psychology
Editor Michael Argyle

Ideology
L. B. Brown

L. B. Brown

Ideology

Penguin Education

Penguin Education
A Division of Penguin Books Ltd,
Harmondsworth, Middlesex, England
Penguin Books Inc, 7110 Ambassador Road,
Baltimore, Md 21207, USA
Penguin Books Australia Ltd,
Ringwood, Victoria, Australia

First published 1973
Copyright © L. B. Brown, 1973

Made and printed in Great Britain by
Cox & Wyman Ltd,
London, Reading and Fakenham
Set in Monotype Times

Contents

For a friend

And for those who write

Mao lives
People's Revol
Vorster kills
University kills
Shoot all racists
Stop living on borrowed time
Fighting for peace is like fucking for chastity
We are the writing on your wall
Etc.

Editorial Foreword

Professor Laurie Brown is well known for his research in the psychology of religion, and is a social psychologist of great erudition and sophistication. Ideologies are systems of beliefs about social issues, which are partly a product of socialization, group membership, social movements and personality. The problems discussed in this book lie therefore at the heart of central concerns of social psychology. Laurie Brown has written a richly documented, well-informed account of an important and relatively unfamiliar part of social psychology. He provides numerous examples of ideologies and of scales for measuring them. At the same time he adds a new dimension to areas such as socialization, personality and group processes. The book is a welcome corrective to social psychological approaches based on trivial experiments. It should also be of much wider interest in helping people to understand how ideologies function.

M.A.

1 The Context

Use of the concept of 'ideology' has become a popular way of referring to the systems of thought and the explanations that underlie many forms of social and individual behaviour. A classic ideological statement is to be found in Unesco's constitution. 'Since wars begin in the minds of men, it is in the minds of men that the defences of peace must be constructed.' Webster's Dictionary defines ideology as 'a systematic scheme or coordinated body of ideas or concepts, especially about human life or culture'. Over recent years we have all learnt to live with ideologies and with ideological differences. They now come in many guises and can describe or characterize the ideas or opinions that lie behind political, social or economic actions. As propositions they become epigrams and slogans to mobilize and confuse groups or individuals. They polarize hostility and antagonism, justify social oppression and persecution, rationalize yet another national or international crisis and confrontation, or generate loyalty and cohesion. It cannot be accident that causes many to regard questions of politics, religion and sex as the critical domains for dispute. They are, therefore, topics to be avoided.

It is commonplace to attribute the 'cold war' to ideological differences, and the concept of ideology sustains and explains differences between East and West (whether in Europe or Asia), North and South (Korea, Vietnam or America), Black and White (in the United States and in South Africa), Right and Left. Ideologies also 'explain' differences between rich and poor, old and young, and between men and women. The precise meaning and content of any of these differences is not always clear, nor are people certain how they may have arisen. While some ideologies grow from a consensus or a tradition, others have been constructed by philosophers or by agents of the mass media. They may be defined in a constitution, a declaration of rights or a treatise, or they must be deduced from communications designed to influence our attitudes and behaviour. Such communications are to be found in newspapers, television programmes or sermons and in the forms of relationship between officials and their clients or between doctors and patients. Ideologies may also be deduced from a man's common assertions, or perhaps from the other responses that he makes. Their clearest forms of expression are linguistic, and so an ideology is an integrated set of propositions about some important social area or domain. Verbally-based measures are therefore appropriate for their study.

Attitudes and beliefs

Any systematic set of attitudes and beliefs, whether about the nature of the universe, political policy, family structure and patterns or family planning, can be 'explained' with reference to a wider ideological content which may in its turn be related to a deeper ideological structure that uses for its terms an appeal to economic factors, reason or emotion, or an appeal to a personality-based process of which the subject may be unaware.

The assumed interaction between the content of an ideology and those who hold it has led to theories about the determining function of personality or cognitive structure in the development of ideology, and in the modes of attachment to a system of beliefs. These theories may be circular. William Temple is reported to have said to a student that, 'It is your personality that makes you say that it is my personality that has caused me to believe in God.' But people certainly differ in the degree to which they are sensitive to defined sets of ideas.

Whatever the explanation, related attitudes and beliefs, opinions and constructions of fact develop around social objects to form patterns from which particular attitudes and behaviours stem. This contingent behaviour ranges from anchored judgements about loosely related issues, to the selective search for confirmatory information, and interpreting or predicting the complex responses of other people. Selectivity and generalization are facilitated by control from an ideological system, although individuals differ in the extent to which they are influenced by, or are even aware of, a defined set of ideas or system of thought. Differences have been found between people in the 'openness' of their cognitive systems (Rokeach, 1960), while those who hold an ideology use group support or previous experience to validate their beliefs. When these sanctions are not available the beliefs tend to change, unless a pseudo-consensus can be found to sustain marginal beliefs.

Ideologies vary in their applicability, explicitness and generality. Will Hanoi, Peking or Moscow negotiate? Should a woman be appointed as a consultant surgeon or a High Court judge? Elaborate answers may be given to these questions, but a simple, direct reply can usually be derived from a general system of belief which is often robust enough to allow predictions or assertions about matters only loosely related to it. This is especially easy when assertions relate to identified groups like the 'working class', 'women', the 'Communist Party', or the 'Left' and the 'Right'. Even in psychology some differences, as between experimental and social psychologists, have been said to be ideologically based.

The uses of ideology

Intergroup conflicts based on ideological differences are not new, although their explicit recognition may be. (Was the great schism between Rome and Constantinople *really* over a trivial matter of one word in a creed?) The invention of 'ideology' is attributed to a French philosopher de Tracy (1754–1836), who, around the time of the French Revolution, claimed to have devised a true analysis of the human mind in the formation of ideas. Among others using the word have been Marx and Engels in their *German Ideology*, Mannheim in *Ideology and Utopia*, and Money-Kyrle in *Psychoanalysis and Politics*.

In the London Bibliography of the Social Sciences, between 1931 and 1955 there is roughly one entry a year under the heading *Ideology*. For the years 1956 to 1962 there are fifteen entries ($2\frac{1}{2}$ a year), and there are seven a year for the period 1962 to 1968. The concept has gained its recent popularity with the current awareness and emphasis on group differences, now that revolutionary change has become a recognized and viable instrument of policy. Systematic work in the social sciences has produced an acute awareness of the political and social environment, a sensitivity to the assumptions that underlie and control society as well as to the analysis of social structures, and to the persons who constitute a society (cf. Ingleby, 1970).

Although the concept of ideology was developed in philosophical and political analyses and is now closely associated with revolutionary thought and action, it has become a fashionable concept among psychologists, particularly for those who have lately discovered cognition and have escaped from the early irrationalism in explanation that Allport (1954) identified and rejected. The role of ideas, beliefs and facts in guiding and directing social behaviour is central to the consistency and congruity theories of attitudes (Feldman, 1966), which stand in contrast to the functional analyses (Katz, 1960).

Ideologies are communicated in the materials of popular culture; notably in the idealization of the military and of crime and violence in comic books and television films, and in a preoccupation with 'sexual permissiveness'. We cannot consider the intentions behind these forms, and it might be paranoid or ideological to try, but we can examine the effects of recognized ideologies on attitudes and beliefs, and on the behaviour of those exposed to them. These effects may be expected to show in the legitimation and definition of particular attitudes, whether positive or negative, and in interests in, or knowledge about, other related areas. Since the members of any society will have ideas, beliefs and opinions about their society's organization and its values, norms of honesty and goodness, freedom and equality belong themselves to an integrated ideology.

Ideologues

Social power rests with those who can control and implement an ideology, whether by persecution and torment or by education and propaganda, while each society contains deviants from whom there is much to be learned about that society. An attack on another's ideology may reflect a pungent ideology in the attacker, especially if either attacked or attacker occupies a minority position. Critics of others in a received social system must exercise care not to step beyond the accepted limits and recognized mechanisms of change. Thus the career of Senator Joe McCarthy is particularly instructive (cf. R. Brown, 1965), as might be that of Mr Enoch Powell or the Rev. Ian Paisley. It was the rise to power of the European fascists that gave impetus to a study of authoritarianism as a personality characteristic (Adorno *et al.*, 1950) and to an explicit psychological analysis of ideology. At the United States subversion trials in the 1950s, in the case against Professor Lattimore, whose name was linked with the post mortems on Far Eastern policy, it was said on 2 May 1953 that 'When public excitement runs high as to alien ideologies is the time when we must be particularly alert not to impair the ancient landmarks set up in the Bill of Rights.' Such a trial, or the involuntary incarceration in mental hospitals or prisons of those who are marginal or deviant, emphasizes the social control that is possible through the sanctions on belief and behaviour. Ideologies interlock and must be carefully unwound for analysis. They also operate with various levels of generality and abstraction and it must be recognized that many people may act or terrorize without any ideological foundation to their behaviour.

Specified for measurement

The detailed description of particular ideologies is not a purpose of this monograph, except as they have been formulated and measured in scales and questionnaires. Some of these are reviewed in chapter 3. Webster's Dictionary refers to 'bourgeois', 'medical' and 'legal' ideologies, and to a 'national ideology'. The ideologies intensively studied by psychologists lie in the political, economic, social, sexual, medical and religious domains, and in the patterns of cultures and of organizational behaviour. All of these not only enshrine ideas and explanations, but entail evaluation and affect, or feelings and wishes. In fact Lifton makes these components the basis of his definition: 'any set of emotionally charged communications about man and his relationship to the natural and supernatural world' (1961, p. 149). The configuration and functional interdependence of these elements is a further important characteristic of them. Since ideologies relate to the content of systems of attitudes and beliefs, a primary psychological interest in the concept has related to questions about their acquisition, maintenance and structure, and to the behavioural processes that are their effects. These interests stand in contrast to the more specific concerns of philosophers, historians or sociologists.

Social behaviour is influenced by interaction with others. These influences include the traditions within which behaviour is structured, as well as the face-to-face encounters. On the other side there are probably some internal, personality-based characteristics, which may themselves have been moulded by social processes. These separated sets of social and individual factors are in continuous interchange, and many studies have concerned their relative importance. In a psychological analysis of ideology, the main concepts are therefore attitudes and beliefs, social and cultural influences, socialization and learning and the personality processes that mediate and actualize social relationships. These personality processes entail cognitive and motivational factors operating idiosyncratically or as shared patterns. But whatever mode of analysing ideologies is adopted, some detachment from society's bonds is necessary for it to begin. The development of an ability to think abstractly about thought and about the social context and its structures is itself a psychological question of some interest which is the broadest aim of this book. The fact that this ability seems to have emerged late in the general history of thought indicates the difficulty of making the appropriate de-centrations.

2 Basic Attitudes and Beliefs

Ideologies have been abstracted from statements of public policy, from doctrines about political issues, religious ideas, moral positions, aesthetic judgements and even from specific social practices. When ideological thought impinges on behaviour, it is expressed so that it can be recognized in attitudes and beliefs. These elements differ in their centrality and in their generality. In the subject index to *Psychological Abstracts*, under Ideology the reference is to 'Value and Values, Attitude'; in the 1968 index, 'Belief' was included as well.

Distinctions between attitudes and beliefs, and between opinions, knowledge, values and stereotypes have not always been well drawn. The concepts are often used loosely so that some beliefs are called 'opinions' and others become 'attitudes'. Concepts like interest, prejudice and norm involve further aspects that have been identified. But each may involve a different 'state of mind' and have its own typical forms of response to issues or social objects. Each certainly implies its own way of being tested, constrained by logic or experience.

Attitudes

Attitudinal responses are usually verbal, but they may be non-verbal emotional predispositions involving feelings. They are therefore evaluative responses. The behavioural implications or translations of an attitude are complex, and do not imply a simple one-to-one correspondence. The majority of measures depend on paper and pencil, verbal techniques. Kiesler, Collins and Miller (1969, p. 21) say, 'Almost every paper using a technique other than self-report is a methodological paper, published just to prove it is possible to measure an attitude without self-report.' They also 'warn' that there is little work that reflects 'the theoretical emphasis on behavioural implications of attitudes' (p. 9). But, if a person declares a positive attitude towards communists and a negative attitude towards conservatives, he can be expected to use predictable words to describe each group and its members, to act consistently towards them, and he may well experience predictable feelings when he is in contact with them. These forms of response can be casually observed, and some of them have been extensively studied under controlled conditions. They are shaped by previous experiences, and because social attitudes define and limit social reality and express coping styles, it is not surprising that there is a vast literature concerned with them. Social psychology has even been defined as the study of attitudes.

It has been objected that this field is top-heavy with theory and that more attention ought to be given to response consistencies in attitude-related behaviour. There have, however, been three broad stages in the development of the attitude concept. It was initially absorbed into psychology from a common use, to refer to the ways in which people set or orient themselves before carrying out an action, whether this was in response to an auditory stimulus or to interpret the meaning of an ambiguous visual figure. The concept then came to refer to a mental process (*aufgabe*), and later it was applied to the responses to social objects and issues. Since about 1930, considerable effort has gone into building satisfactory measures of social attitudes. Recently the main work has moved to attitude change and consistency.

Everybody carries general or specific attitudes to a wide range of social issues and objects, and some controversy has centred on the ways in which they are organized, whether directly in terms of their verbal content or more abstractly as predispositions in, for example, 'radical' or 'conservative' attitudes. Attitudes can certainly be grouped by their content, and the measures usually involve a presentation of some specific attitude content. But because of differences in the salience or intensity of the attitudes across different areas, and the fact that knowledge of an object is not required before an attitude develops, attitudes have also been interpreted as personality styles, or as expressions of involvement and commitment. So authoritarian social attitudes and positive religious beliefs have been attributed to personality, despite the fact that they may also be tightly anchored in social roles, social expectations or in some reference group.

Formal definitions of attitudes are either operational, or descriptive and interpretative. Operational definitions rely on the observed consistencies of behaviour; so Campbell (quoted in Green, 1964) defined an attitude as 'an enduring syndrome of response consistency with regard to a set of social objects'. A very persistent but interpretative definition has been that advanced by Allport (1935). His definition breaks down into five aspects, so that attitudes are (a) a neural and mental state, (b) of readiness to respond, (c) organized, (d) through experience, and (e) exerting a directive and dynamic influence on behaviour. With this definition, an attitude becomes a latent variable or an underlying process, and the 'readiness to respond' is a readiness either to make actual responses or to construct and interpret the social world in characteristic ways. A person with positive religious attitudes would be expected to interpret his world differently from someone with negative religious attitudes, and differently from one who is strongly disposed to political action. The fact that attitudes are organized implies recognizable linkages between their elements, and the form of these attitude structures could be crucial when the relationships between attitudes and ideologies are considered. Ideologies are, in their turn, organized.

A less cognitive emphasis has concentrated on the dynamic role of attitudes in fixing meaning and directing attention to certain classes of stimuli. A further view relies on explicit formulations (including ideologies) and treats attitudes as learned responses that take their meaning in the context of a wider system. In one of Asch's studies (1952, chapter 15), the statement, 'I hold it that a little rebellion, now and then, is a good thing, and as necessary in the political world as storms in the physical', was read by subjects who were either told it had been made by Jefferson, or by Lenin. These different attributions altered the whole context and produced entirely different interpretations of the statement's meaning. Other work has shown that attitudinal or belief states influence the rate at which material relevant to some attitudes is learned (Morlan, 1950).

Attitudes also influence social responses and control contact between groups. Campbell (1967), in a discussion of stereotypes as rather fixed attitudes, shows that groups have a high degree of mutual responsiveness. In one example he notes that the English describe themselves as reserved, and respecting the privacy of others and that they would describe 'Yankees' as intrusive, forward and pushing. Yankees, in their turn, describe the English as snobbish, cold and unfriendly and themselves as friendly, outgoing and open-hearted. In a similar way, a person might describe his own social group as showing pride, self-respect and reverence for tradition, while an out-group would be egotistical, self-centred and clannish. Points of reference are important in the evaluations and descriptions that are made: to one interest group a course of action might be progressive, while the same action would be paternalistic to another. Inter-group conflict and misunderstanding often rests on such interpretations. In a similar way, a person's own position on an issue strongly influences his ratings of a range of statements about that issue (Hovland *et al.*, 1957; Scott, 1962). In contrast to psychological interpretations, there are other theories which assume that the significance of attitude rests, for example, in what is concealed (the *interest* theory) or in their inadvertent functions (the *strain* theory) (cf. B. O. Brown, 1968).

Beliefs

Beliefs refer to the probability dimension of an attitude or concept, and differences between attitudes and beliefs have been specified in terms of the separate operations involved in each. Fishbein and Raven (1962) proposed a form of generalized scale in which a concept (like communist) was to be assessed along a series of bi-polar semantic scales, including 'harmful–beneficial', and 'wise–foolish' to give an attitude measure and an 'impossible–possible', 'false–true' for a measure of belief.

These belief scales involve assent to the truth or probability of a proposition or statement, while the attitude measure is evaluative. Attitudes may simply be disagreed with, but beliefs are falsified when the reality does not correspond with assertions made about it.

Thouless (1935) showed that there are differences in the item-operating characteristics of different kinds of belief. A tendency was found for greater certainty about (untestable) statements of religious beliefs (e.g. 'there are such spiritual beings as angels') than about statements of 'fact', like knowing the year in which Mary Queen of Scots was beheaded, or whether there are tigers in China. Beliefs are not necessarily equally testable.

As an example of the extent to which attitudes and beliefs are interrelated, in a recent unpublished study, sixth formers in a Wellington secondary school were asked to express their own attitudes to each of forty-two social issues from the Wilson–Patterson conservatism scale. Each subject was then asked to predict the responses of four others in the class – the two people whom he knew best and the two known least well. These predictions relate to beliefs about the others. The results showed greater certainty for each subject's own attitude response, rather less certainty about the responses of his best-known friends and uncertainty about those whom he knew least well. Values, on the other hand, relate to a simple preference between equally possible alternatives. *Nonsense*

Attitude theories

Cognitive explanations of attitudes have stressed their importance in providing information about the social world and in facilitating interaction with it. The functional or adaptive theories treat attitudes as expressions of underlying psychological needs.

In line with a cognitive theory, Krech and Crutchfield (1948) list the dimensions along which attitudes differ. These include direction and extremity, salience, differentiation and action orientation. To this list might be added conviction and resistance to modification or change. Katz and Stotland (1969) suggested simply the number of elements, their degree of structure, fluidity and extensity. These classifications suggest the forms of analysis that are possible for defining attitude structures.

Following the work of Heider (1958), it is now common for attitudes (as well as interpersonal and social relationships) to be analysed in terms of their balance, congruity or consistency (Abelson, 1968; Feldman, 1966). When the attitude elements are imbalanced, implicit pressure to change is assumed. This imbalance may derive from actual inconsistencies between the elements or with related behaviours. The efforts to produce consistency produce a state in the person that motivates him to make changes in the attitude elements or in his behaviour. We won't examine the details of these models of attitude structuring, but can note that there are numerous examples in the everyday expressions of attitude and ideologies of apparently inconsistent statements being tolerated and of an excessive strain towards consistency. Bertrand Russell's use of the word 'compossibility' (as a 'possible coexistence with something else', OED) has some advantages over these other concepts. In his *Autobiography*, Russell writes that

among the desires that a man finds himself to possess, there are various groups, each consisting of desires which may be gratified together and others which conflict. You may, for example, be a passionate adherent of the Democratic Party, but it may happen that you hate the presidential candidate. . . . The art of politics consists very largely in finding as numerous a group of compossible people as you can (1969, pp. 33–4).

Tawney enunciated a similar principle when he observed that, 'the heart of man holds mysteries of contradiction which live in vigorous incompatibility together' (1926, p. 212).

Katz (1960), on the other hand, advanced a functional theory of attitudes and identified the four roles which attitudes fulfil as adjustive or instrumental, ego-defensive, value-expressive and to give understanding or meaning through a knowledge of the world. This functional analysis recognizes the ambiguity in any expressions of attitudes, and the fact that they become integrated responses.

Attitude change

A continuing interest in attitude studies has been in the nature and possibility of their change (e.g. McGuire, 1969). Many attitudes are acquired during one's socialization and acculturation. They involve learning to make appropriate responses towards social objects, whether as a result of direct example or as a generalization from behaviour in other situations. If a child consistently experiences hostility, or sees it directed towards minority groups, a foundation will be given for attitudes that accept treating others in this way. The balance between actual behaviour, abstracted generalization and understanding is a fine one. Social influence and related role behaviour, as well as specific examples, all contribute to the acquisition of consistent attitudes, and the structured ideas and expectations that go with them.

Attitude change among adults involves responses to propaganda and persuasion, as well as to subtle social influence. A large body of work now relates to the many separate aspects of this process, but it is hard to integrate them to make good predictions about how attitudes are likely to change under real conditions. Communications and messages, direct interaction and new information are all likely to have potent effects, while extreme forms of social control during interrogation have been used to produce change, especially in ideologies. 'Brainwashing' is usually applied to those influences to change that are disapproved, and one explanation of its effect has been by the use of Pavlovian concepts (Sargent, 1958). 'Thought reform' has been blamed for facilitating the recognition and spread of some extremist ideologies, especially during the last twenty years or so. Lifton (1961) describes milieu control, mystical manipulation, the demand for purity and the cult of confession among the specific techniques used in brainwashing. More benign sources include the influence of mass media, direct social contact and derivation from other principles. Whether changes in attitudes and beliefs will occur probably depends upon the techniques used, in relation to the content and the centrality of the issues that are made the subject of direct influences. McGuire's analysis of the components in attitude change follows Lasswell's summary by specifying what is known about the effects of 'who says what to whom, how, and with what effect' (McGuire, 1969, p. 172).

Attitude acquisition and change are not necessarily conscious processes. We come to like the things we believe and are inevitably influenced by the ideas that circulate in our environment. Particular situations also have effects on expressed attitudes, and so people may fail to act as they say they will, and verbally stated attitudes have not been found to relate closely to actual behaviour (La Pierre, 1934). Perhaps there must always be discrepancies between actual behaviour and what is thought or believed, so people have said one thing and done another, like preaching transcendental values and pursuing materialistic goals, or talking about doing good while doing others down. With so many constraints at work on social actions, and the many possibilities of response that range between verbal prejudice and physical violence, political and social attitudes are usually thought to have their coherence in an ideology, and not in some essentially irrational process or in the actual forms of behaviour. They are certainly available as verbal responses, about which there are differences in the amount of consensus.

Beliefs, on the other hand, are influenced more by reasoning and experience than by indoctrination: Sarbin, Taft and Bailey (1960) list induction, construction, analogy and authority as the sources of beliefs. Doubt and disbelief are of course other states that emerge from similar processes.

There can be no doubt of the importance of the actions that people will engage in as a consequence of their beliefs and attitudes: yet these behavioural consequences are difficult to demonstrate under controlled conditions in experiments. These consequences range from accepting imprisonment or martyrdom, to continued witnessing and uncomfortable campaigning. Such is our scepticism of course that these effects are dismissed on some motivational grounds rather than accepting them as stemming from an intellectually accepted position. The evaluations and assessments of the behaviour of others is open to many ideological distortions, and the distinction between public and private expressions needs to be made strongly. Kiesler (1971, p. 13) gives a 'phenomenological analysis' of ten reasons why a person faced with a request for action might not act. He suggests that in general 'people are wary of explicit and attitudinally relevant behaviour because it is restricting in its implications for the future.' Translating an ideological stance into action suffers from the same defects, and an ideology may be more use as a mechanism to evaluate the behaviour of others than as a plan for action. Despite the relative neglect of social action, some behaviours and experiences do have direct effects on attitudes (cf. the attitudinal effects of varying the severity of initiation, Aronson and Mills, 1959).

Therefore ...

The objects of attitudes are other people, social issues and social groups. As an evaluative process, attitudes adjust the responses to social objects, and individual attitudes result from the effects of social influences and from group memberships. Although attitudes and values can lead to complex behaviours like power-seeking, authoritarianism and punitiveness, they are usually measured through verbal responses to particular objects. Some of the measures that are ideologically relevant will be discussed in the following chapter, but ideologies themselves become social objects. Philosophies, faiths, myths and even morality are other objects of attitudes.

Attitudes simplify the making of social responses and, like concepts, they are linked together in coherent systems. Attitudes also link with social and personal factors to form the external and internal components of behaviour. Unresolved questions concern the importance of distinctions between general social attitudes (like humanitarianism or radicalism) and their specific content or the objects to which they necessarily relate, and the beliefs and actions that are related to them. Disapproval of free immigration *because* it would cause a lower standard of living shows such a belief contingency. A general consensus about some beliefs may produce rigid attitudes, and beliefs and attitudes become closely intertwined and balanced together.

Social responsiveness is in general mediated through the beliefs and attitudes that focus on issues and other objects of the social environment. Beliefs refer to a cognitive, knowledge process; to an estimate of probable occurrence. Attitudes refer to the affective, evaluative processes that are involved. These responses are all learned and tend to persist, but are subject to alteration and change, and may spill into action.

3 Specified for Measurement

'Do you agree with the statement that, "Political power grows out of a barrel of a gun"? Does the fact that the assertion was made by Chairman Mao Tse-Tung alter your reaction to it?' Questions like these, or attitude statements to be rated for the strength of agreement, form the items in most of the scales designed to measure attitudes to many social objects, issues and ideals.

The process by which an individual responds to an attitude statement has been simulated in Abelson's 'Ideology Machine' (1968, p. 311). In this computer model an initial belief structure is built for a simulated individual, and organized horizontally as a set of stored sentences, like 'Communist bloc countries interfere economically with neutrals.' Each sentence has an evaluation attached, and the sentences are nested vertically into abstractions about, for example, countries or forms of interference. The programme is activated by the input of a sentence that is constructed from a dictionary list of recognized elements, and the system responds by accepting or rejecting the input assertions, and giving a reason from its information store of sentences or beliefs. A denial process is initiated when an input assertion embodies an inconsistency, as when a 'good' actor performs 'bad' actions. There is also a credibility test which searches vertically for supportive evidence. Abelson has noted that his programme is inefficient and needs improvement, but it does simulate one way that real subjects may set about responding to the statements in an attitude scale.

Development both of the general methods of attitude measurement and of particular scales has been closely related to advances in attitude theory. The central role that the concept of 'attitude' has occupied in social psychology depends largely on the available and agreed methods of measurement and the scales that have been built to assess a very wide range of specific attitudes.

Attitude scales

Recent collections of attitude scales have been published that describe and evaluate many of the acceptable measures. Shaw and Wright (1967) consider 176 scales, while the University of Michigan's Survey Research Center has produced three volumes that cover measures of political, occupational and social psychological attitudes. Many of the scales considered in these volumes are relevant to questions of ideology (Robinson, Rusk and Head, 1968; Robinson, Athanasiou and Head, 1969; Robinson and Shaver, 1969). Since progress must depend on agreement about markers that can be used in further studies, attitude scales are evaluated against accepted criteria of reliability and validity, of item construction and response set, or as Robinson and Shaver say, against 'psychometric criteria (representative sampling, presentation of proper normative data, test–retest reliability, item homogeneity, discrimination of known groups, cross-validation, and further statistical procedures)' (1969, p. 4). Once a specific variable or construct has been defined, items to assess it are collected or constructed, and the best ones are identified by pre-testing. At a later stage, group membership and voting behaviour may be used as external criteria to validate the scale, although there are lots of assumptions involved in this procedure, and convergent validation across measures may be preferable.

Robinson and Shaver (1969) deal with 106 scales in their volume on social psychological attitudes. The main areas they cover are life satisfaction and happiness, self-esteem and self-concept, alienation, authoritarian and dogmatic personality characteristics (this is the largest section and covers 27 scales), political scales including nationalism, social responsibility and a new left scale, values, described as 'meta-attitudes', i.e. 'constructs that are more over-arching and pervasive than attitudes', general attitudes towards people, religious attitudes, and finally the measures of social desirability that control for response sets. They excluded measures of achievement aspiration, conformity, marital and family attitudes and social-personality characteristics. As an adjunct to specific measures, Remmers (1934) developed some generalized scales that might in principle be used to measure attitudes to *any* practice. These have now been largely replaced by the semantic differential as a general method of measurement (Osgood, *et al.*, 1957).

The forced or closed responses to a set of attitude statements are simple to score, in contrast to the difficulties of coding material from a free and less constrained expression of beliefs and opinions obtained in free interviews, or by analysing the answers to specific but open questions like 'What do you think of war?' or 'What gives in religion?' Answers to these questions are hard to analyse because the replies may be unreliable, and are inevitably biased by such extraneous factors as the context in which they were asked, the time available for answering them and the subject's own readiness to respond to, and expectations about, the interviewer. There are always limits on self-disclosure, and strong pressures work towards giving socially acceptable responses. The items that are to form a scale are first identified by their content and may be later subjected to a factor analysis or other item analysis to purge them and isolate a pure dimension.

Scaling procedures

Many attitude concepts are defined largely by their measures, and any measures imply a specified underlying dimension or variable. While an available scale may need to be refined, and even to have its items renovated from time to time, the actual scaling procedures that were early developed have not been superseded. Questionnaire methods are to be found in the work of Galton, but the first formal scale was Bogardus's social-distance scale (1925), which is still in use. Thurstone's method for calculating scale values for attitude statements (1928) was a major advance. He adapted the assumptions and methods of classical psycho-physics and built scales to measure an underlying dimension, defined by a consensus among a group of judges who are asked to evaluate the favourability of each statement or item towards the issue being scaled. Likert's much simpler summated rating scale method (1932) was found to give scores that correlated highly with the results from Thurstone's more laborious procedures, and it has now become the most common form of attitude measurement. Likert's method asks respondents to show their agreement with each of a series of statements by applying a five- or seven-step *a priori* scale (for example, agree strongly, agree slightly, neutral, disagree slightly, disagree strongly). Arithmetic weights are assigned to each step on the scale, and a total score is obtained by summing the weighted replies for each item or statement, provided that the items in the scale have been found to be homogeneous. It has been argued that the neutral category in a Likert scale may be ambiguous, because there are different reasons for neutrality. But in one study (L. B. Brown, 1962a) two kinds of uncertainty were made available, and this was found to have no effect on the final results. These subjects were able to mark either 'the statement is as likely to be true or false', or 'uncertain because of lack of information or interest'.

Other methods include Guttman's cumulative scales (1944), the semantic differential scales devised by Osgood *et al.* (1957), and Sherif's *et al.* (1965) use of latitudes of acceptance and rejection which recognizes that an attitude may refer to a range of possible responses. These methods all rest on scoring or weighting the subjects' responses to a set of defined items, as stimuli. The actual form of response is specified by the particular set of instructions for a scale, and they commonly require a simple expression of acceptance or rejection of each statement, or showing the magnitude or strength of agreement or of belief or disbelief. The scores calculated from these patterns of answers allow comparisons to be made between subjects, once the scale has been found to satisfy the accepted scale criteria.

In addition to the content-based scales, some attention has been given to assessing attitudes indirectly, using response measures that do not depend on a deliberate response to any item's explicit content. Examples include measures of change in physiological reactivity through pupil size or skin conductance (Woodmansee, 1970), measuring speed of response as an index of conviction, yielding to the social pressure imposed by a member of some identified group in an autokinetic situation as an index of prejudice, and analysing the 'errors' made in answer to apparently factual questions to assess attitudinal bias (Weschler, 1950), or assessing factual knowledge as indicative of interest. Webb *et al.* (1966) have discussed further examples of these non-reactive and indirect measures.

Despite the continued effort to devise content-free measures of attitudes, some content must be used as the stimuli in studies of beliefs and ideology. This content must be carefully identified, and usually rests on some method of content analysis to produce a set of well-defined categories. Stone *et al.*'s General Inquirer (1965) is an example of a computer-based system for content analysis in which a series of look-up functions is executed by a categorizer which classifies the elements of a passage into constructs that have been specified by a prior dictionary. Rokeach has developed another kind of dictionary as a method for assessing the relative importance of values that express sets of instrumental values about modes of existence, and terminal values or goals. In a recent paper (1970), Rokeach has used his scheme to identify the authors of disputed documents (see page 160). The main difficulty in any content analysis is to recognize what may be irrelevant and can therefore be discarded and to establish comparable categories among subjects. This problem is related to the fact that the meaning of some specific content may be clear only when its context is known (which may include knowing what is intended). But any method for gathering data has some limitations, which is one reason why Campbell and Fiske (1959) argued for the use of convergent validation by multi-trait multi-method procedures in which several different measures are used to assess a single variable. It is obviously impossible to validate introspective data except by some convergence across measures.

Scott (1969) has developed objective forms of analysis to assess the 'natural cognitions' of individual subjects, using a set of ten measures. These methods have many possible uses, beyond their initial application to nations and to concepts of self. The repertory grid methods have also attempted to give each subject the opportunity to apply his own constructs (like 'sincere', 'prejudiced') to concepts or 'elements' (Fransella and Bannister, 1967). This approach rests on G. A. Kelly's theory of a 'personal construct system' which is the individual's own organization of his social environment.

Content analysis

One advantage of data derived from a content analysis of documents is the fact that they are not changed by the demands of an investigator, and written materials often express ideological content directly. So a detailed analysis of the moral pressures and social doctrines in the evangelical hymns can clarify some of the ideologies with which Sunday-school-reared children were frequently confronted (Sangster, 1963).

Party political statements are also often explicit in their ideological content. A well-recognized problem in them is the extent to which words like democracy, freedom, revolution and reform are used as slogans, often in a restricted and special sense to elicit stereotyped responses. (A conservative candidate in Australia wrote in a pamphlet on Liberalism and Trade Unionism that 'there is no freedom without freedom of choice, and when this freedom is threatened that is when the Liberal and the Socialist clash'.) What a thing is to be called, and the differences between denotative and connotative meanings (Snider and Osgood, 1969, pp. 131–5) allow plenty of room for disagreement, and for detailed studies of meaning. In everyday behaviour there are many subtle ways of expressing an ideological content beside verbal expressions. But beyond the exploratory stages of a psychological inquiry, the use of carefully written items as stimuli is generally preferred to the simpler procedures in which responses cannot be controlled.

In general, the more complex the task a subject is given, the greater is the information that can be extracted from the responses, but also the more sophisticated will be the subjects to whom the task is relevant. For this reason alone, the subjects of many studies have been 'captive' students. A few brief scales have been used in large social surveys of the general population, whether by personal interview or by mail. Postal surveys always suffer from a lack of cooperation and barely two-thirds of a sample can be expected to reply, even under the most favourable conditions. Promises of anonymity do not seem to increase the number of replies that are received. In two recent postal studies in New Zealand, I found that 53 per cent of those on a church's roll returned a questionnaire relating to beliefs about prayer, while 59 per cent of a random sample of trade union members returned questionnaires about their beliefs and attitudes to their union.

Although survey questionnaires often use single items rather than sets of scaled items, single-item tests are very unstable, and longer tests give better reliability. One single item that might work is a kind of riddle: 'A man was driving his son to school when they were involved in a bad accident. The father was killed, the boy was badly injured and rushed to hospital. The surgeon took a look and exclaimed, "Oh, it's my son!" How could this be?' Imprisoned in a male-dominated society we do not easily realize that women can be surgeons (Jones, 1970) or that men can be nurses (Etzkowitz, 1971). Once the range of content of a variable has been established, certainties and linkages begin to characterize its operation as an ideology. There are also constraints. A Catholic may be prepared to argue about physics but not about family planning. His access and his attitudes to these issues differs, as does his involvement with them.

Item wording

Anyone who wants to develop his own scale or questionnaire, or who intends to use an available scale, should become acquainted with the principles and the methods of attitude-scale construction. It is not enough simply to throw together a few items and hope or expect them to work. A scale must be well based theoretically, carefully pre-tested and well evaluated. Accounts of the methods of scale construction can be found in Edwards (1957), and in Coombs (1964). Even with the greatest care, scaled items age. This has been a barrier to the continued use of the same content-defined measures, although a few, like the F-scale, have continued to be used extensively. The wording of items is critical. Fishbein, for example, discusses how the statements 'Negroes are happy-go-lucky' and 'Negroes are intelligent' might be equally good measures of attitude to negroes, granted that they are appropriately interpreted (1967, p. 261). A minor alteration to the wording of an item can change its meaning and operating characteristics. Robinson, Rusk and Head (1968, p. 11) cite their attempt to simplify the item, 'It is the man who starts off bravely on his own who excites our admiration' to 'We should all admire a man who starts out bravely on his own'. The original item measured individualism, but in the altered form it was closely associated with authoritarianism. Sets to respond to positively worded items must also be corrected. The simplest correction for this acquiescence is to switch the direction of some items and make them negative. But it is not always easy to write negative items: Rokeach (1967) has even argued that the authoritarianism items cannot be reversed without altering what they measure. Edwards (1957) advocates that all items should be calibrated for their social desirability and matched in forced-choice pairs. Despite the subtle efforts to guard against some deliberate faking of responses, this can't be eliminated entirely, which is why detailed interviews have been found necessary to supplement rather bare attitude responses. Another alternative is to give subjects an opportunity to suggest alterations to the wording of any statements they dislike. When this opportunity was given to the subjects in a study of their religious beliefs, I found that 49 per cent did not make any comments on the item wording, and that most who did make comments disagreed with the form of the items, or referred to their limited application.

In the domains of religion and politics and in relationships between the sexes, ideological systems have become obvious guides to behaviour. They also have a role in sensitizing us to general issues, especially when these involve persecution or injustice directed towards recognizable groups. Of the many ideologies that could be described, only a few have been subjected to psychological study with good scales available to

measure them. Different ideologies are not necessarily empirically separate, and questions of the interrelatedness of ideologies
continually recur, either through concepts like the dogmatism
that is associated with a firm stance, regardless of the particular
content, or with ideological content generalized to represent
positions along Left or Right, Traditional or Modern, and
Conservative or Liberal dimensions. Antonyms seem to exist
for any position that can be identified on an issue, whether it is
about reform, race, war, man and his environment, population
growth, inflation, crime, drugs, civil disorder, morality, work,
Scientology, political manoeuvring to recognize China, and so
forth. Many people adopt positions that are not neutral on these
issues, and it is such stands that make measurement possible.
Individuals can then be compared. People also differ in their
detection of ideologies as well as in their commitment to them.
Even the 'end-of-ideology' thesis (Waxman, 1969) itself
becomes an ideology to foster stability and traditional processes. But events change many issues. Fluoridization and the
recognition of China might be examples, although some are
still fighting these issues and others, like censorship.

It is hard to capture all the aspects of an ideology when
making measures, and classical formulations like those of
Machiavelli or Rousseau, Marx or Freud might give good
leads. Christie and Geis (1970) explain how informal specula-
tion about successful interpersonal manipulation was combined
with the insights of Machiavelli (1469–1527) to yield items for
a series of internally consistent questionnaires to measure the
predisposition to interpersonal manipulation. In a rather
similar way measures of the authoritarian personality were
developed from modifications of attitude items that had been
used in the 1930s, supplemented by insights from detailed
interviews with prejudiced individuals on both the extreme Left
and the extreme Right (cf. Shils, in Christie and Jahoda, 1954).
Weber formed a thesis about the relationship between protestantism and the rise of capitalism, and isolated the ideology of
a Protestant Ethic. Others prefer to rely on implicit formulations
and will castigate officials (and others) for exemplifying a
recognizable ideology in their behaviour, whether of 'racism'

or 'sexism'. Public figures also contribute to the reservoir of ideologies by their statements.

Psychological analysis has tended to emphasize the ideologies that concern interpersonal relationships or conflicts, especially in political ideals, social differentiations and in values. There has been almost no psychological concern with ideologies about property.

A few psychological concepts have contributed directly to ideological analyses. These include security, autonomy or responsibility in social power, and inner or outer control. But whatever the form of the analysis, it exposes opinions and myths about the ideals of a society, and about the norms of social behaviour.

Scale construction

The main steps in constructing an attitude measure involve specifying the issue to be measured, selecting items for it from various sources, and writing new ones. Items come from common opinions about the issue, unless it can be defined with reference to a creed or a platform, or from a body of writings. The pool of items is sorted, pre-tested, judged for relevance, and the poor items are discarded. When the best items that cover an issue have been identified, they can be administered to appropriate subjects. The results are then scored and checked for reliability, and for validity. Subsequent refinement is aimed to produce a uni-dimensional scale, and to explore relationships with measures of other variables. Although a scale may have been built to assess a single ideology, it will not necessarily be psychologically simple because, while the items tap a single domain of ideas, they may not have a single psychological core.

Some actual measures

To exemplify the methods of measurement, some of the typical scales will be described. The ones that have been chosen show different approaches to the ways of formulating measures of ideologies. The first few give examples of rather simple scales. The later ones relate to some of the more general ideologies or orientations that have been explored. Psychologists have approached ideologies in a variety of ways, and many measures of the believed content and of the strength of attachment to an ideology have been developed. Content studies rest on an initial identification of an ideology in freely expressed responses, or through answers to closed questions. Use of free responses presupposes that the ideological material is recognized and available. But ideologies differ in their explicitness and in the extent to which as a general stance they can spill into dogmatism and similar styles. Since an ideology can facilitate closure, the form in which it is believed may be quite different from its formal or official statement.

Beliefs about mobility. In analysing upward social mobility, Turner (1966) refers to the sets of beliefs about mobility as ideologies or 'a collective phenomenon to be distinguished from the study of individual attitudes'. He described the American pattern of contest mobility as 'like a sporting event in which many compete for a few recognized prizes. The contest is judged fair only if all the players compete on an equal footing'. This he contrasts with 'sponsored mobility, the English pattern, (which)... favors a controlled selection process. In this process the elite or their agents, deemed to be best qualified to judge merit, choose individuals for elite status who have the appropriate qualities'. To assess these ideologies, he constructed several situations *a priori*, like the following one that relates to 'standard mobility'. 'An intelligent boy, from an *ordinary working-class family*, wants to become a research scientist. Do you think it is good to encourage such ambition in a boy from a working-class family?' He used three other similar situations and for each there was a further question, like, 'Now, thinking about the same boy from a working-class family: if he has the necessary ability, what do you think are his *realistic chances* of becoming a research scientist?' The eight questions were answered by national samples in Britain and the United States, and the results indicated equal approval for any mobility that follows customary channels, but 'greater approval of irregular mobility, and generally greater confidence for successful mobility in the United States'.

There was in this study no attempt to scale the replies, and the hypotheses were tested against simple and direct questions that *seemed* to Turner to bear on them.

Political ideology. A very common use of 'ideology' is illustrated by McClintock and Turner's (1962) study of 'impact of college upon political knowledge, participation, and values'. They use the term 'political ideology' interchangeably with 'political attitudes and ideas'. Twenty items were used as measures of 'the degree to which students felt that the Federal Government should increase its involvement in highways, education, medical care, employment, business and electric power', and for issues relating to civil rights, 'ethics in government, the distribution of power within government, the regulation of labour unions, etc.' From the answers to these items, three indices were formed for '(a) civil rights, (b) Federal power and (c) an overall index of liberalism-conservatism'. This use of 'ideology' is rather different from that which relates it to the elements of a specific philosophical or religious system – unless one grants that the American political system is based on some identifiable, coherent and well-formulated principles.

This study also illustrates the common strategy of assessing change cross-sectionally, in this case by comparing the replies of Freshmen and Seniors. The authors are well aware of the hazards in this method, and they conclude from the political ideology items that 'It is evident from the nature of the responses given to the political attitude items that this college population reflected a middle-of-the-road political philosophy', and that the 'Freshmen and Seniors did not differ in political knowledge, involvement, or ideology'. Waterman and Waterman (1971) use 'political ideology' in an even more general way and do not cite the interview questions that they used for its assessment. Their study explores the ways that 'political and religious ideology' changes as adolescents move into adulthood.

Need achievement. McClelland developed a system for scoring the strength of achievement motivation from the stories that are given to the stimulus pictures of the Thematic Appreciation Test (Murray, 1938). This scoring system basically gives a count of the number of achievement-related ideas or themes expressed in stories like the following,

The boy is taking an hour's written (exam). . . . The test is about two-thirds over and he is doing his best to think it through. . . . He will try hard until five minutes is left, then give up, go back over his paper, and be disgusted for reading but not learning the answers (McClelland, 1961, p. 41).

One use of McClelland's analysis has been to relate the concept of need achievement to Weber's hypothesis linking protestantism and its ideal of self-reliance with the development of capitalism. McClelland notes that 'The Protestant Reformation might have led to earlier independence and mastery training, which led to greater *n* achievement, which in turn led to the rise of modern capitalism' (1961, p. 47). Measures of need achievement allow a test of the hypothesized link between this ideological system and its psychological effects. Because the measure is based on a projective test, an unaware subject would find it hard to distort or deliberately falsify his replies unless he could guess how the scoring would be done. Projective methods stand against the more common methods that use scaled verbal responses to measure ideologies, and the link between this projective method and an ideology is through the synthesis of need achievement with Weber's theory.

A simpler approach to the measurement of Weber's concept of the Protestant Ethic was adopted by Lenski (1963, p. 89). He asked his subjects directly about their work-related values, and had his subjects rank in order of importance five values, including 'high income' and 'the work is important and gives a feeling of accomplishment'. The latter alternative is thought by Lenski to be 'closest to the Protestant Ethic as conceived by Weber'. Lenski reports that nearly half of those he interviewed ranked the Protestant-Ethic alternative first, that the rankings were related to class, and that white protestants had the greatest number who placed this alternative first. The essence of the Protestant Ethic is described by Lenski as individualism and competitiveness, and these are also characteristics of the middle class. The working-class patterns of thought are, he says, 'collectivistic and security-oriented' (1963, p. 113). Lenski's method stands at an extreme from the indirect projective method used by McClelland. Perhaps the ideals of self-indulgent protectiveness can be contrasted against productivity and constructiveness, but subtler methods than were used by Lenski would seem necessary to measure them, and to relate them reliably to class membership. This difference illustrates the definitional problems that arise when deciding how to construct adequate measures of an ideology and in even deciding what is to be called an ideology.

Values. Many commentators have identified coherent systems of values in cultural and in personal terms. De Tocqueville described Americans as preoccupied with freedom, egalitarianism and physical well-being. Fromm and Riesman dealt with the emergence of a marketing- or other-directed personality, as a value-related orientation. Gorer has treated generosity, hatred of authority, concern with interpersonal relations and the acquisition of money as values. Other value analyses have been deduced from documents, inferred from communications in the mass media and derived by questioning individuals (e.g. Scott, 1959). Scott (1965) described eight personal values and their corresponding international goals, so that self-control corresponds with pacifism, intellectualism with cultural development, kindness to people with humanitarianism, social skills with coexistence, and so on.

Probably the best-known test for measuring values is the Allport-Vernon-Lindzey *Study of Values*, although Robinson and Shaver (1969) list eleven other measures of values. The *Study of Values* was based on Spranger's analysis of the six types of personality that are expressed through values or evaluative attitudes. The crux of the typology is set out in the Manual to the Test, where it is said that Spranger 'does not allow for formless or valueless personalities, nor for those who follow an expedient or hedonistic philosophy of life'. The *theoretical* value is aligned with 'the discovery of truth', the

Eric Boyton,
Chief Technician, 0 dpt.

economic value with an interest 'in what is useful'. 'In his relations with people (the economic man) is more likely to be interested in surpassing them in wealth than in dominating them (*political* attitude) or in serving them (*social* attitude). The *aesthetic* man sees his highest value in form and harmony. The social man is characterized by a "love of people".' 'The political man is interested primarily in power', and 'the highest value of the *religious* man may be called unity.' It is emphasized that these are 'ideal types', and that a given person cannot be expected to belong exclusively to one type. Questions were written to assess each value by itself and in comparison with others, so question ten in Part II asks, 'At an evening discussion with intimate friends of your own sex, are you more interested when you talk about (a) the meaning of life (*religious value*); (b) developments in science (*theoretical*); (c) literature (*aesthetic*); (d) socialism and social amelioration (*social value*)?' These alternatives are to be ranked, and a weight of four is given to the most preferred alternative. The test has been used widely in research, and the examples of specific studies referred to in the Manual include differences between recognized groups, changes in values over time, resemblances between friends and family members, and the way in which values are related to differences in perceptual and cognitive functions.

As a different method, Klućkhohn and Strodtbeck (1961) developed an interview method that is aimed to measure dominant and variant value orientations in different cultures, using solutions to twenty-two common human problems in situations like the following:

Two men spend their time in different ways when they have no work to do. One man spends most of this time learning or trying out things which will help him in his work. (This is the *doing* orientation.) One man spends most of this time talking, telling stories, singing, and so on, with his friends. (A *being* orientation.) Which of these men has the better way of living?

Ideological labels. If the assumption is made that labels to specify an ideological stance (like 'communist' or 'christian') become integrated into a person's identity and self-description, it is relatively easy to assess the availability and the use of these labels by asking subjects to write, say, twenty separate answers to the question, 'Who am I?'. The 'Who am I?' or 'Twenty Statements' test (Kuhn and McPortland, 1954, in Robinson and Shaver, 1969) has been used to assess the salience of a religious identity and could also be used to measure political identities or the ways that role-related behaviour takes shape. Many factors will influence the use of such labels, but the technique could allow for the identification of those people in a large group who might be intensively followed up to establish the detailed content of their underlying ideologies, or whatever similarities there might be in their background. Adults can be expected to exhaust salient consensual identities (like student, girl, studying engineering) before mentioning subconsensual traits (like happy, bored, good student) (Robinson and Shaver, 1969, p. 141). It is not clear when membership and ideological identifiers would typically emerge.

The salience of ideologies as concepts could also be assessed by Harvey's 'This I Believe' test which involves sentence completions (1970). In this test subjects are asked to indicate their beliefs about specified referents (like marriage, religion, majority opinion) by completing in two or three sentences the phrase 'This I believe about marriage . . .' (or about 'religion' or 'majority opinion'). Completions are to be scored along critical dimensions, like specific–abstract, or for signs of immediacy and detail.

Religious ideologies and beliefs. As well as using ideological labels (including denomination), there are several scaled measures of the separable components of a religious attachment or position. There is a current controversy about the dimensionality of these measures, and whether the theoretically separable components of religion (as orientations to belief, or across different doctrines) lie on one or more dimensions. Dittes (1971) gives an extended analysis of questions about 'the degree of differentiation between religion and other phenomena' and about 'the degree of differentiation within religion.'

A serviceable measure of christian religious-belief strength includes the following items (Brown, 1962b):

1. Matter is the sole reality (with scoring reversed).
2. There are such spiritual beings as angels.
3. Jonah was swallowed by a great fish and afterwards emerged alive.
4. Christianity is a better religion than Buddhism.
5. The Bible is literally true in all its parts.
6. There is a Hell in which the wicked will be everlastingly punished.
7. Right will triumph.
8. There is no life after death (with scoring reversed).

Alienation. Among the concepts that have emerged from sociological theorizing is Durkheim's notion of anomie, described as 'a state of mind in which the individual's sense of social cohesion – the mainspring of his morale – is broken or fatally weakened' (quoted by Merton, 1968, p. 216). It merits attention not only because it has been widely used but because it connotes an absence of ideology, or of normlessness. Robinson and Shaver (1969) have reviewed fourteen separate scales for its measurement, of which Srole's (1956) five-item Anomia scale is probably the best known (Robinson and Shaver, 1969, p. 175). The statements in this scale are each to be rated for a simple 'agree', 'disagree', or 'can't decide'. The range of scores is 0–5 because unequivocal agreement with any item scores +1. The five items are:

1. There's little use writing to public officials because they often aren't really interested in the problems of the average man.
2. Nowadays a person has to live pretty much for today and let tomorrow take care of itself.
3. In spite of what some people say, the lot of the average man is getting worse, not better.
4. It's hardly fair to bring children into the world with the way things look for the future.
5. These days a person doesn't really know whom he can count on.

These items are rather transparent and it may be surprising that the percentages cited by Robinson and Shaver as agreeing with them are respectively 39, 29, 33, 23 and 50. Robinson and Shaver also reproduce the following negatively-worded items that Christie suggested might offset the response set to agree:

1. Most people can still be depended upon to come through in a pinch.
2. If you try hard enough, you can usually get what you want.
3. Most people will go out of their way to help someone else.
4. The average man is probably better off today than he ever was.
5. Even today, the way that you make money is more important than how much you make.

Not only can the items be reversed to correct for response sets, but the direction of the whole scale can be changed: Berkowitz and Lutterman (1968) identified 'the traditionally socially responsible personality' as the opposite of alienation, as it involves a 'sense of participation and involvement in one's community and society'. Their eight-item Likert-type scale is as follows:

1. It is no use worrying about current events or public affairs; I can't do anything about them anyway.
2. Every person should give some of his time for the good of his town or country.
3. Our country would be a lot better off if we didn't have so many elections and people didn't have to vote so often.
4. Letting your friends down is not so bad because you can't do good all the time for everybody.
5. It is the duty of each person to do his job the very best way he can.
6. People would be a lot better off if they could live far away from other people and never have to do anything for them.
7. At school I usually volunteered for special projects.
8. I feel very bad when I have failed to finish a job I promised I would do.

Srole's five-item scale has been used in a study of the assimilation of Latvian migrants in Australia, since Taft (1965, p. 156) proposed it as a measure for the 'secondary integration' and satisfaction of migrants. Three items, concerning the disinterest of public officials, not knowing who to count on and another item covering the belief that 'most people don't care what happens to the next fellow' each had significantly more Latvians than Australians responding in the anomic direction (Jaunzems and Brown, 1972). Sears (1969, p. 406) has summarized US studies concerning 'alienation and migrancy'. Scores on alienation have been used as dependent measures in many other studies (e.g., Turner and Lawrence, 1965), and to examine whether those having a 'conservative personality' are alienated and hostile. The general conclusion is that there are different kinds of alienation and of political conservativeness. 'Some people espouse conservative views because in their groups such attitudes permit the expression of strong underlying hostile trends. For other people, conservatism reflects adherence to the ideals of their segment of society.' This ambiguity is at the heart of the psychological analysis of any ideology.

Authoritarianism and the F-scale. An intensive interest in ideologies among psychologists can be dated from the publication in 1950 of the *Authoritarian Personality*, by Adorno, Frenkel-Brunswick, Levinson and Sanford. This marked a turning point, not only because of its direct effects in formulating a theory and giving scales of measurement that have been widely applied, but also because it stimulated a lot of constructive methodological and theoretical criticism (Christie and Jahoda, 1954; Kirscht and Dillehay, 1967).

Two main problems with the F-scale concern its specific ideological content and the problem of acquiescence in response to its items. The original scale consisted of items that were all associated with authoritarianism of the right (e.g. 'It is only natural and right (*sic*) that women be restricted in certain ways in which men have more freedom'). The recognition of this defect led to attempts to measure some other general patterns like dogmatism (Rokeach, 1960).

The original authoritarianism scale was worded for positive responses, so that endorsement of all the items yielded a high score. The scale therefore did not differentiate between a response to the ideological content and a set to agree regardless of the particular item content (cf. Peabody, 1966; and Rokeach's 1967 argument against the response set interpretation). This is a complicated issue that is yet to be fully resolved, but it has evidently proved difficult to write good reversed F-scale items, and, although acquiescence may itself be confounded with authoritarianism, it may also be an inherent component of authoritarianism.

Despite its recognized weaknesses, the *Authoritarian Personality* established unequivocally that there are links between some social attitudes and personality processes. The personality theory adopted by these authors was broadly psychoanalytic, and the study argued that attitudes can serve irrational, ego-defensive functions (see page 136). Forerunners of this theory can be found in the 1930s with the work of Stagner, Edwards and Maslow, and of Fromm who was linked with Horkheimer and the *Institut fur Sozialforschung* in Frankfurt, which itself played an important part in formulating the ideology behind the whole study. Adorno *et al.* (1950) describe the elements in the authoritarian personality: these cover attitudes of anti-semitism, ethnocentrism, political and economic conservatism, idealization of parents and self, anti-introception, rigid sex-roles, concern for status and the cognitive styles of rigidity and intolerance of ambiguity. These nine variables are described in detail by Adorno *et al.* (1950, p. 228ff.), and their main measures used Likert's technique, with a seven-point rating scale. The actual scales covered (a) anti-semitic ideology. (A-S) with five sub-scales, (b) ethnocentric ideology (E) with three sub-scales, (c) politico-economic ideology (PEC), and (d) the fascism scale (F).

In addition to the data from these scales, other material was gathered with a series of factual questions, from projective questions (like 'What would you do if you had only six months to live, and could do anything you wanted?'), from Murray's Thematic Apperception Test and from clinical interviews. A further criticism of the whole study has been the contamination in the analysis of this 'clinical' material.

The final forms of the original scales are long. To illustrate the items, the following brief ten-item form of the F-scale was tested and used in Australia (L. B. Brown, 1962a):

1. Obedience and respect for authority are the most important virtues children should learn.

2. No weakness or difficulty can hold us back if we have enough willpower.

3. Every person should have complete faith in some super-natural power whose decisions he obeys without question.

4. What youth needs most is strict discipline, rugged determination, and the will to work and fight for family and country.

5. Young people sometimes get rebellious ideas, but as they grow up they ought to get over them and settle down.

6. Sex crimes, such as rape and attacks on children, deserve more than mere imprisonment; such criminals ought to be publicly whipped, or worse.

7. People can be divided into two distinct classes: the weak and the strong.

8. There is hardly anything lower than a person who does not feel a great love, gratitude and respect for his parents.

9. If people would talk less and work more, everybody would be better off.

10. No sane, normal, decent person could ever think of hurting a close friend or relative.

Robinson and Shaver (1969, chapter 5) have set out some other modifications, including forced-choice versions, reversed items to try and control for acquiescence, and a brief four-item form.

The validity of the analysis of attitudes in the *Authoritarian Personality* has been tested against studies of known criterion groups. Analyses of the content of statements and speeches of identified fascists have further reinforced these results, and other background material is discussed in Shils' account of

Right and Left in authoritarianism (Christie and Jahoda, 1954, pp. 24–29).

That the concept of authoritarianism is still alive is shown in a study by Kagitcibasi (1970) who compared Turkish and American samples, and concluded that, while authoritarianism is a coherent syndrome in the US, it is not so in Turkey. Obviously any set of attitudes must be available within a culture before it can be used to express personality functions.

Derivatives from authoritarianism. There have been three main developments. Eysenck (1954) was able to extract two factors, radicalism–conservatism and tough-mindedness–tendermindedness (following a distinction made by William James) from political material. His analysis identified radicalism on the right as tough-minded and on the left as tender-minded – but Eysenck's work was itself severely criticized (see Rokeach and Hanley, 1956; Christie, 1956a; and Eysenck's replies, 1956).

Rokeach and Hanley criticized Eysenck's empirical and theoretical work of the 'tough-mindedness–tender-mindedness' dimension for the errors they found in his data and especially in the item analysis over the criterion groups. They would have preferred a 45 degree rotation of this factor to align it with the factors earlier identified as religionism and humanitarianism. Christie pursued other methodological points that related primarily to the sampling procedures and to the items themselves. It is tempting to speculate that the acrimony of this argument, fuelled by Eysenck's replies, may have been due in part to some extraneous feelings that surrounded the issues themselves. The debate shows clearly some of the problems that surround item wordings and validation, and has not yet been settled, as Green and Stacey (1964) show.

Rokeach (1960) developed scales to measure dogmatism as closed-mindedness, and opinionation on both the right and the left. Robinson and Shaver consider that this dogmatism measure may not identify radicals of the left well enough, despite the fact that it implies a cognitive style or form of response rather than any particular content. There is also Christie's work on Machiavellianism that began from his observation that, while the F-scale correlates negatively with education and social status, there are bigots and interpersonal manipulators to be found throughout any social system; and the use of social power can be seen as a specific kind of authoritarian behaviour.

Rokeach argued (1960, p. 13) that a difficulty with the theory that guided both the research on authoritarianism and its measuring instruments was its neglect of all but fascist authoritarianism. He also argued (1967) that the response-bias criticisms against these attitude scales is inadequate and, more importantly, that it is inadvisable to use reversed items to measure authoritarianism since both 'authoritarians and anti-authoritarians can be confidently expected on theoretical grounds to generally agree with reversals, which are always worded in a democratic direction.' Distinctions between content and structure can be quite clearly drawn from ideological systems, and questions about the general predispositions that link personality into these structures are important. The way that a person holds his beliefs defines his intolerance more than do the things that he actually believes. As Rokeach says, 'We have observed them (the intolerant) in religious circles and in anti-religious circles, in the academic world where the main business at hand is the advancement of knowledge' (1967, p. 13). Rokeach therefore developed a politically neutral Dogmatism Scale, designed 'to measure individual differences in the extent to which belief systems are open or closed', and two opinionation scales 'designed to measure individual differences in the extent to which we accept and reject others depending on whether they agree or disagree with us' (p. 20). These scales therefore measure general intolerance on both the left and the right.

The Dogmatism Scale was based on an analysis of the organization of belief–disbelief systems and has a central–peripheral and a future–past time orientation as subsidiary dimensions. There are in all sixty-six items in the scale, which as Rokeach says 'covers a lot of territory'. Items assessing belief–disbelief include, 'the United States and Russia have just about nothing in common', those measuring the central–

peripheral dimension are a constellation of 'pre-ideological' primitive beliefs, e.g. 'Man on his own is a helpless and miserable creature', and the time-perspective items include, 'The present is all too often full of unhappiness. It is only the future that counts.' Although the dogmatism scale scores correlate with both the left and the right opinionation scales, they are more closely related to right than to left opinionation, while the scales all have a weak but consistently positive relation with conservatism (1960, pp. 126–7). Rokeach's principal explanation of these facts is that communism, unlike fascism, is humanitarian in its ideology or *content*. He concludes that the psychological functions of communist beliefs may differ from those of fascist beliefs, citing as evidence the disillusionment that he believes occurs more often among former communists than among former nazis or fascists.

The opinionation scale consists of forty deliberately constructed double-barrelled statements, like 'Only a simple-minded fool would say there is a God', and 'Any intelligent person will tell you that God exists.' These statements give information about the subject's belief in God and a judgement about whether he accepts those who agree with him. The scale items are balanced so that half are worded for agreement to express left opinionation and the other half to express right opinionation. The prescription for assessing the items follows:

First conjure up statement Á, which is the ideological opposite of statement A. Then judge whether statement A is to the left or the right of statement Á. Proceeding in this way, it is possible to decide easily and objectively, regardless of one's own ideological biases, whether a given ideological belief is politically to the left of center or to the right of center (p. 82).

Recent work with these scales has been described by Rokeach (1967) and the concept of dogmatism is reviewed by Vacchiano, Strauss and Hochman (1969), who found general support for the validity of Rokeach's concept and evidence for a 'dogmatic personality' style.

Another derivative from the *Authoritarian Personality* is Christie's analysis of Machiavellianism. As he says,

The personality description of those scoring high in ethnic prejudice and professing right-wing political ideology rang intuitively true to me. These were familiar characteristics to one who had spent his early life in the Bible Belt. There was, however, one aspect of Shils' critique which also rang true. He pointed out that extremists of the political right, with rare exceptions, were extremely ineffective in political movements. Their very extremity of ideology coupled with a concomitant inflexibility of political tactics, did not permit them to make the compromises which are necessary for political success (Christie and Geis, 1970, p. 2).

The characteristics of the 'smooth operator' were identified as (a) a relative lack of effect in interpersonal relationships, (b) a lack of concern with conventional morality, (c) a lack of gross psychopathology and (d) low ideological commitment.

Although Christie and Geis (1968) deny that their measure of Machiavellianism (or Mach) is ideologically oriented and assert that it deals with interpersonal tactics, it does relate to a kind of ideological disposition. While Christie and Geis report an average correlation of -0.10 with authoritarianism, they argue that 'High scorers on both scales should agree with a simple statement, "Most people are no damn good." Underlying the F-scale, however, is a moralistic and judging predisposition: "Most people are no damn good *but they should be*;" whereas a high Mach might say, "People are no damn good, why not take advantage of them?"' The difference between Machiavellianism and authoritarianism may be a difference between opportunistic and moralistic responses, while Machiavellianism may assess an interpersonal social skill.

The Mach items were derived from the writings of Machiavelli converted to statements that would fit a modern opinion inventory. As an example, Machiavelli's assertion that 'Most men mourn the loss of their patrimony more than the death of their fathers' was edited to read, 'Most men forget more easily the death of their father than the loss of their property' on the grounds that this didn't change the basic meaning and the revision would be more meaningful to current populations (Christie and Geis, 1968, pp. 961–2). Some new items, like 'Barnum was probably right when he said there's a sucker born every minute', were found not to work as well as those based on Machiavelli's formulations.

The Mach scales have been used with several criterion groups, and consistent relationships have been found between Mach and age, sex, success in college and university, and medical specialization (psychiatrists have high Mach scores while surgeons and obstetricians produce the lowest score). Christie concludes from his correlational studies that endorsement of the items is not 'systematically correlated with known measures of psychopathology, political ideology or social class', that 'the greater the involvement of an individual in a complex of formalized role relationships with others, the greater the endorsement of manipulative tactics', and that 'College students who were selected as subjects for laboratory studies succeeded in out-manipulating their partners roughly in proportion to their agreement with Machiavellian precepts' (1968, p. 969).

Three versions of the scale are of interest. Mach IV is a Likert-type scale (e.g. 'The best way to handle people is to tell them what they want to hear', 'When you ask someone to do something for you, it is best to give the real reasons for wanting it, rather than giving reasons which might carry more weight', 'Anyone who completely trusts anyone else is asking for trouble', 'It is hard to get ahead without cutting corners here and there', and 'Honesty is the best policy in all cases'). Mach V is a forced-choice form with items grouped in threes. The subject's task is to choose the items he thinks are the most characteristic and the least characteristic of himself. In each triad, one item is a buffer, another item is keyed for the scale and is matched in rated social desirability with a third unrelated item. If the keyed and matched items are high in social desirability, the buffer is low, and vice versa. The subject, confronted with an innocuous positive buffer, agrees with it and then chooses one of the other two items as least like him. This is a very sophisticated way of controlling for both response set and social desirability, and Christie has found that his subjects could not fake responses when they were asked to do so. One triad in Mach V reads:

A. It takes more imagination to be a successful criminal than a successful businessman.

B. The phrase 'the road to hell is paved with good intentions' contains a lot of truth.

C. Most men forget more easily the death of their father than the loss of their property.

(A is weighted 1·95, B 3·60, and C weighted 1·95 is the Mach alternative.) There is also a 'Kiddie Mach Test' (Christie and Geis, 1968, p. 327) with items like, 'It hurts more to lose money than to lose a friend'.

Levinson's scales and some other ideologies. Daniel J. Levinson, who was involved in the original studies of the authoritarian personality, has developed further scales to assess ideologies in political, religious and social domains. In 1944, he had published with Sanford an anti-semitism scale, where anti-semitism was defined as 'an ideology, that is, as a relatively organized, relatively stable system of opinions, values and attitudes concerning Jews and Jewish–Gentile relations'. In that scale they deliberately used negatively worded items to avoid assessing a self-righteous tolerance. Levinson considers that ideology is 'a relatively organized, relatively stable pattern of thought within the individual, and is an aspect of personality'. Each individual chooses from the externally available alternatives and those selected become organized 'on the basis of his personal cognitive–affective motivational modes of functioning'.

Levinson and Huffman (1955) devised a scale to measure 'traditional family ideology' in which, as they put it, 'ideological orientations regarding family structure and functioning ... are placed along an autocratic–democratic continuum.' The autocratic extreme is represented by an emphasis on discipline in child-rearing and a sharp dichotomization of sex roles, while the democratic orientations decentralize authority within the family, seek equality in relationships and maximize individual self-determination.

Apart from merely constructing another scale, Levinson and Huffman aimed to explore consistencies in a particular stand about some issues of social life, since an 'individual's family ideology is related to, and enmeshed within, a broader orientation towards social institutions generally', and 'a man's approach to any aspect of organized social life, such as the family, is intimately bound up with his conception of self, his modes of handling anxiety and his character traits'. Holding this family ideology should be related to authoritarianism, and that theory guided the scale's construction. They recognize that the scale content will be bound by the 'particular traditions, social pressures, range of available ideological alternatives and idiomatic meanings' of the American middle class. The psychological variables that are incorporated involve conventionalism, authoritarian submission, exaggerated masculinity and femininity, extreme emphasis on discipline and moralistic rejection of impulse life. The scale itself is a seven-point Likert type, with three levels of agreement and three levels of disagreement. The scores on it are related to the California Ethnocentrism and Fascism scales ($r=0 \cdot 65$ and $0 \cdot 73$ respectively) to religious preference and practice, and to the answers to a series of projective questions about the ideals of a good husband, wife, and child, and to belief about modes of child-rearing. An abbreviated twelve-item form of the Traditional Family Ideology scale contains the following items:

1. Some equality in marriage is a good thing, but by and large the husband ought to have the main say-so in family matters.

2. If children are told much about sex, they are likely to go too far in experimenting with it.

3. Women who want to remove the word *obey* from the marriage service don't understand what it means to be a wife.

4. The most important qualities of a real man are determination and driving ambition.

5. A child should never be allowed to talk back to his parents, or else he will lose respect for them.

6. A man should not be expected to have respect for a woman if they have sexual relations before they are married.

7. It is somehow unnatural to place women in positions of authority over men.

8. The family is a sacred institution, divinely ordained.

9. A woman whose children are at all messy or rowdy has failed in her duties as a mother.

10. If a child is unusual in any way, his parents should get him to be more like other children.

11. There is hardly anything lower than a person who does not feel a great love, gratitude and respect for his parents.

12. The facts on crime and sexual immorality show that we will have to crack down harder on young people if we are going to save our moral standards.

There are several other scales designed to measure family ideologies, some of which are listed by Straus (1969).

Gilbert and Levinson (1956) constructed a scale to assess a 'custodial mental illness ideology'. This concept has been important within the mental-health field, since there are differences in the approaches and theories about mental illness, not least in conflicts between psychiatrists, psychologists, other professional groups and the 'general public'. The items in this scale include the following:

1. Only persons with considerable psychiatric training should be allowed to form close relationships with patients.

2. It is best to prevent the more disturbed patients from mixing with those who are less sick.

3. As soon as a person shows signs of mental disturbances – he should be hospitalized.

4. Mental illness is an illness like any other.

5. Close association with mentally ill people is liable to make even a normal person break down.

6. We can make some improvements, but by and large the conditions of mental hospital wards are about as good as they can be considering the type of disturbed patient living there.

7. We should be sympathetic with mental patients, but we cannot expect to understand their odd behaviour.

8. One of the main causes in mental illness is lack of moral strength.

9. When a patient is discharged from a hospital, he can be expected to carry out his responsibilities as a citizen.

10. Abnormal people are ruled by their emotions; normal people by their reason.

Gilbert and Levinson found that in two differently oriented psychiatric institutions, a custodial orientation towards treatment was related to authoritarianism, and that occupational groups within the institutions differed in their typical responses. It seems clear that ideology and beliefs about mental illness influence attitudes towards those who are mentally ill. Cumming and Cumming (1957) found in their well-known attempt to change attitudes towards mental illness in a Canadian community that sound information had the effect of reinforcing existing (unfavourable) attitudes and norms, and they were unable to effect a change towards better informed opinions.

Strauss *et al.* (1964) have identified three psychiatric ideologies: psychotherapeutic, somatic-therapeutic and socio-therapeutic. These ideologies may reflect different professional identities and training, and models of the 'illnesses' are derived from physical medicine, from a psychological explanation (including learning) or from social, legal or political terms. The differences are potent, and institutions as well as those who work in them can be identified from the positions that they adopt. Strauss *et al.* (1964) found that, while individual experiences with the mentally ill were related to ideologies, professional role commitments and the institutional structure both accounted for more variance than did actual interaction with patients. The mentally ill are too often treated in ways that are consistent with an ideology rather than as individuals. This is an important area in which ideologies and beliefs influence judgements about people. Freeman and Giovannoni (1969) noted that the value orientations of research workers have specific effects on their studies of ideology in mental illness. 'Social psychologists generally have sought to expose authoritarianism and bureaucratic arrangements, and most of them are personally committed to a therapeutic community and a psychodynamic point of view. Given this situation, it is often hard to judge the extent to which interpretations of their studies are a function of personal ideology or a consequence of empirical findings.' It is clear that 'mental illness' is a socially defined characteristic, about which people come to have strong preconceptions. These attitudes derive less from what the mental patient *does*, than from his having been labelled as 'mentally ill' (Freeman and Giovannoni, 1969).

Thomas and Sillen (1972) have catalogued some opposing judgements or interpretations about racial differences in the United States which relate to such areas as intelligence (they stigmatize Jensen's argument as racist), family relationships, sexual behaviour and fantasies. As an example of their stance, they criticize psychoanalytic interpretations of 'racist violence' originating in the infantile unconscious or in Oedipal relationships. They say, 'This mode of explanation reduces the event to an exercise in psychodynamic abstractions. The persons taking part in the violence appear as mythic symbols that might as well represent the bloody happenings in ancient Troy as the confrontation in Detroit' (p. 115). In a similar way they note that 'The concept that deviation from the conventional norm is pathological becomes manifest in the readiness to label student activists and black militants as emotionally disturbed' (p. 141). There are obviously many subtle pressures towards reinforcing the power of an Establishment, among which they include psychiatry. They go on to note that 'The therapist cannot assume that his own training has given him an objectivity that guarantees freedom from all racist ideology and feeling' (p. 144).

Cohen and Struening (1962) administered a scale of opinions about mental illness to professionals and to semiprofessionals and in a factor analysis of the results they found five dimensions of attitude: authoritarianism (the largest factor), benevolence, mental-hygiene ideology, social restrictiveness and interpersonal ideology. A distinction can be drawn between opinions about mental *illness* and about mental *hospitals*. Answers to questions about hospitals carry some institutional components and are aligned with other institutional ideologies – about the military, schools and universities, and about the Church. So Levinson also has a religious conventionalism scale (1954) and an internationalism scale (1957). Both deal with the elements of institutional control.

Psychologists' ideologies. Differences among the orientations of psychologists are quite well recognized, although they are not always treated benignly. The 'humanistic' psychologists, for example, call themselves a third force in psychology, to emphasize their study and understanding of 'the person as a whole', in contrast to the approaches by behaviourists or by psychoanalysts who constitute the other 'forces'. Each of these groups criticizes the others, and so Eysenck (1972) and Laing, each from his own position criticizes Freud. Laing (1967) has become the apostle of the psychotic ideology and in his later writing he celebrates the schizophrenic condition and the mystical apprehension of those who are psychotic. The normal person is alienated, while the psychotic has 'broken through' to reality. Buhler (1971) argues for the humanistic study of single cases, and for the recognition of an identifiable core in them. Although the humanistic psychologists are not alone in this plea, the events in any life history must be interpreted from a particular theory and a 'life history' itself implies some simplification. Throughout the history of thought, many different bases and theories have been advanced to explain the threads in behaviour (see Burnham, 1968). Recent controversies about Skinner's ideology of behaviour control further emphasizes some of these ideological disputes (1972).

Students are not always sensitive to the explicitly ideological implications of some of the psychology they read; nor are they aware of the psychologism implicit in some psychological theories. The common psychological research ideology of naive empiricism may be being replaced, especially in Germany, by what Holzkamp calls the 'constructivism' that has emerged from a modification of Popper's notion of falsification (Mortenson, 1972).

Two contrasting paradigms of human nature can be identified. One is an ideology of control that, as Miller (1969) says, 'has great appeal to an authoritarian mind, and fits well with our traditional competitive ideology based on coercion, punishment and retribution.' The other is based more on assumptions of flexibility and constructiveness. To exemplify these ideologies, Miller (1969) summarizes the current conceptions of man that were described by Varela:

Our current social paradigm is characterized as follows: All men are created equal. Most behavior is motivated by economic competition, and conflict is inevitable. One truth underlies all controversy, and unreasonableness is best countered by facts and logic. When something goes wrong, someone is to blame, and every effort must be made to establish his guilt so that he can be punished. The guilty person is responsible for his own misbehavior and for his own rehabilitation. His teachers and supervisors are too busy to become experts in social science; their role is to devise solutions and see to it that their students or subordinates do what they are told.

For comparison, Varela offers a paradigm based on psychological research: there are large individual differences among people, both in ability and personality. Human motivation is complex and no one ever acts as he does for any single reason, but, in general, positive incentives are more effective than threats or punishments. Conflict is no more inevitable than disease and can be resolved or, still better, prevented. Time and resources for resolving social problems are strictly limited. When something goes wrong, how a person perceives the situation is more important to him than the 'true facts', and he cannot reason about the situation until his irrational feelings have been toned down. Social problems are solved by correcting causes, not symptoms, and this can be done more effectively in groups than individually. Teachers and supervisors must be experts in social science because they are responsible for the cooperation and individual improvement of their students or subordinates (p. 1070).

It seems likely that the different approaches to psychology may fit with consistencies in other social attitudes. Hudson (1970) has described how school-leavers intending to study in arts or in science differ in their opinions or stereotypes about those who are already active in each field. He found that the 'scientist' is perceived as intelligent but cold, dependable but dull, valuable but lacking in imagination. The arts specialist in contrast is warm but undependable, exciting but relatively unintelligent, imaginative but lacking in value. These stereotypes involve structured meanings and Hudson discusses the ways that many students of psychology have tended to react against a rigidly empirical view of the subject. He notes that his students 'find neither pleasure nor enlightenment in the works of the more empirically minded authorities I draw before their gaze'. Furthermore, the students are, as he says,

alert to the social and cultural processes; not only in 'society', but within systems of knowledge. . . . And they take it for granted that the credo on which I myself was weaned – psychology as the science of behaviour – is either at the descriptive level a mistake, or an utterance of covert ideology . . . that both linguistic philosophy and behavioural psychology are part of a capitalist plot designed to prevent students from asking searching questions, not merely about the nature of their own discipline, but about the roots of power in the society in which they find themselves.

These attitudes arise partly from the expectations that students bring to their study of psychology. Whether they come with liberal attitudes or are made liberal by their studies is a question of some current interest. But any responses like these are based on prejudices, and those who succeed in a disciplined study may be those who will conform to the implicit norms. A recognition of these norms comes as part of the academic socialization, and has been studied in some schools of professional training, especially in medicine (e.g. Becker *et al.*, 1961).

Conservatism. Closely allied to the concept of authoritarianism is the dimension of liberalism–conservatism. Although this dimension has been widely used as an explanation of differences in political (and other) attitudes, Robinson, Rusk and Head (1968, p. 79) assert that 'repeated samples of the national electorate by the Survey Research Center have convincingly demonstrated that no such organizing dimension or ideological structure exists for most citizens. Correlations between specified issue items were often low and, when such congruence occurred, it was generally for other reasons than that of ideology (i.e. most usually a result of self-interest or group preference).'

The concept of conservatism is defined either with reference to the content of attitudes or to a more general predisposition. A simplified item content has been used in the Wilson–Patterson Conservatism Scale (1968). Whereas most opinionation statements have a mean number of words per item around eighteen (Rokeach, 1967, p. 351), Wilson and Patterson reduced their items to only one or two words that can refer directly to each of fifty issues. Wilson and Patterson show that Eysenck's item 'Unrestricted freedom of discussion on every topic is desirable in the press, in literature, on the stage, etc.' can be reduced simply to 'censorship', with 'Yes', ' ?' and 'No' as the alternative answers that are available. Similarly, Stacey and Green's (1968) complex item, 'If the rich were made to share their wealth, then everyone would be a lot happier, including the rich who have more money than is good for them anyway', can be reduced to 'Socialism' with the same alternative answers. Other items in Wilson and Patterson's scale are 'death penalty', 'evolution theory', 'school uniforms' and 'striptease shows'. A general conservatism factor has been found to emerge 'conspicuously' from this fifty-item scale (Wilson, 1970), although there were also racial, sexual freedom and religious factors identified.

A different approach to a conservative ideology is described by Robinson, Rusk and Head (1968, pp. 91–3). This is a five-item scale based on the 'ideological' tenets of conservative political belief expressed by Senator Goldwater in his campaign for the Presidency in 1964. Results are reported from 1397 whites in a national cross-section interviewed prior to the 1964 election, and a 'substantial correlation was found between scores on the index and votes for Goldwater.' The items they used are:

1. The Federal government is gradually taking away our basic freedom. Do you agree?

2. In the past twenty-five years this country has moved danger-
ously close to socialism. Do you agree?

3. Which of the statements on this card comes closest to ex-
pressing how you feel about the state of morals in this
country at the present time?
They are pretty bad, and getting worse
They are pretty bad, but getting better
They are pretty good, but getting worse
They are pretty good, but getting better
Don't know, or the same as ever.

4. How great a danger do you feel that American communists
are to this country at the present time – a very great danger, a
great danger, some danger, hardly any danger, or no danger?

5. Do you feel the United States is losing power in the world
or is it becoming more powerful? If losing power: how much
does this disturb you – a great deal, somewhat, or very little?

Sears (1969) notes that 'society currently socializes young
people so as to give them slightly more liberal beliefs than their
predecessors had'. In a review of the sources of illiberalism, he
emphasizes the place of status and education, and the traditional
American ideas and values, especially those to be seen in
religion. Sears concludes that 'The clearest evidence about the
social origins of illiberal ideas is that they result from socialization in lower-status, less-educated, fundamentalist Protestant, Republican, small-town or farm circumstances' (1969,
p. 413).

Both conservative or liberal points of view can be generalized,
or they may be centred on a particular person or movement (in
the way that Goldwater was able to express and activate a
right-wing ideology). A radical group in New Zealand, the
Progressive Youth Movement (PYM), recently distributed a
strongly worded Youth Manifesto, consisting of eighteen
phrases that detailed current social and political issues which
have consistently aroused intensely negative responses from
the PYM. It began 'Damn your war/Damn your petty morality/
Damn your closed eyes when a peasant's guts spill into

Vietnam's bomb-soaked soil – and open wide when someone says damn. Damn your wealthy churches all praying for the hungry and getting fat.' Mrs Gay Maxwell (1971) reported a comparison of three forms of attitude measure that she derived from this manifesto. One involved rewriting it in non-emotive language. This proved difficult because of the emotional content inherent in the protest and its contrasts between We and They. Another version tempered the language but retained the We/They contrasts, and a third version set out a coherent narrative. Responses to these three forms and to the original manifesto were compared, under the hypothesis that emotiveness of wording would increase the favourability of the responses of those who scored high on a neutrally worded form and would decrease the favourability of the responses of low scorers on the neutral form. Examples of the different forms are set out below:

PYM (original)

18. You offer us your world. It stinks – and you aren't making it any better so Damn off – and let us try – we are the young and it's our world.
13. Damn your lies, hypocrisy, split tongues, double standards.
 2. Damn your petty morality.
 1. Damn your war.
 3. Damn your closed eyes when a peasant's guts spills into Vietnam's bomb-soaked soil – and open wide when someone says damn.

We/They form

18. You offer us your world, it is bad, and you aren't improving it. Stand aside – let us take over – we are young and it is our world.
13. We reject your hypocritical lying and double standards.
 2. We reject your petty morality.
 1. We reject your war.
 3. You are hypocrites when you close your eyes to peasant's blood being spilled into Vietnam's bomb-soaked soil, but open them when someone swears.

Least emotive form

18. Youth should be allowed to reorganize the system they will have to live under.
13. Society is full of double standards and hypocrisy.
2. Accepted morality should be rejected.
1. The war in Vietnam is wrong.
3. It is contradictory to reject obscene language and minor infringement of rules when permitting the atrocities in Vietnam.

Prose argument

We are young. We are restless. We want a chance to make a world in which we can live in honesty and in faithfulness to ourselves and to others. We cannot live freely while surrounded by the hypocrisy, the selfishness, the unrealistic attitudes of this world.

The hard reality of ugly pain in the Vietnam war hurts us. But what hurts us more is the inability of others to see that the proceedings of this war are inconsistent with the personal code of morality which most people would be quick to affirm. On top of this is the frustration we feel when we try to tell people of this discrepancy and they attack our method and ignore our meaning.

The results showed that, although it was impossible to achieve an exact parallel between the items, the manipulations of styles did have some effects on the responses. The more pejorative the wording of the items, the greater was the tendency to disagree with them, and the (reasoned) prose argument produced the most favourable responses. There was also a greater variance of response towards the emotive than towards the neutral versions.

One conclusion from this study is that, while statements can be formulated in basically cognitive terms and do elicit responses, these responses are influenced by the actual *wording* of the items. This effect has been noted already in restatements of F-scale items since the original content produced acquiescence that overlaid any cognitive responses to the item content itself. Wilson's method of merely presenting the bald issues may reduce some effects of bias, but evaluation of an issue may also be an inherent part of any response to it (cf. Osgood *et al.*,

1957). Much more work is needed on the effects of different kinds of item-wording (cf. Bormuth, 1970).

As an example of the extent to which issues, and so item-content are time-bound, one can take a scale that Christie devised to assess the ideology of the New Left. The items were derived from open-ended responses given by Columbia University students arrested during demonstrations in the Spring of 1968 and from New Left publications (Robinson and Shaver, 1969, p. 386). Christie's items were:

1. 'The Establishment' unfairly controls every aspect of our lives; we can never be free until we are rid of it.
2. You can never achieve freedom within the framework of contemporary American society.
3. The United States needs a complete restructuring of its basic institutions.
4. A mass revolutionary party should be created.
5. Authorities must be put in an intolerable position so they will be forced to respond with repression and thus show their illegitimacy.
6. The solutions for contemporary problems lie in striking at their roots, no matter how much destruction might occur.
7. Disruption is preferable to dialogue for changing our society.
8. Even though institutions have worked well in the past, they must be destroyed if they are not effective now.
9. The structure of our society is such that self-alienation is inevitable.
10. Sexual behaviour should be bound by mutual feelings, not by formal and legal ties.

The content of these items is rather different from that of earlier conservatism measures, and from the authoritarianism scale items.

Conservatism is a general ideological stance. McClosky (1958) identified three clusters or factors in conservatism: lower intelligence, a cluster of social-psychological attributes or socially based traits like security, belonging, isolation, worthlessness–inferiority, and a set of clinical-personality processes including poor adaptation, being hostile, suspicious, rigid and compulsive. In general, he found conservative people to be social isolates, with poor opinions of themselves, suffering disgruntlement and frustration. They were said to be generally bewildered by the alarming task of having to thread their way through a society which seems to them too complex to fathom. This structure, he argues, develops like the structure in any ambiguous field, is influenced by indoctrination and group influence, and involves the process of projection which 'creates' a set of perceptions that express, or are consonant with, existing needs and impulses. These factors all contribute to establishing similarities between congenial personal beliefs and the doctrines of an ideology.

Warr, Schroeder and Blackman (1969) examined the conservative political orientation, and showed that it is linked with authoritarianism, tough-mindedness and ethnocentrism as personality factors. They emphasize that their studies are based on response content. There is also the question of the 'structure' of conservatism, in the sense of a generalized organization of belief–disbelief systems along an open–closed dimension having as its elements interdependence among the parts, openness to new information, and the existence of contradictions.

In many analyses of personality and attitude structure, concepts like category width (or breadth), and issue centrality are used, as well as the concepts relating to cognitive consistency. Warr *et al.*, note the major role that has been given to complexity–simplicity which also involves a differentiation across separate dimensions, articulation or the fineness of discrimination along a dimension, and integration across the available dimensions. Some domain specificity might be expected to define the complexity of any individual's attitude structures. Warr *et al.*, analysed data relating to nations separately for left- and right-wing students using paired comparisons, free descriptions and semantic differential assessments. The political orientation of these subjects did not influence the number of dimensions they used to conceptualize the differences between nations, but the left and right subjects differed in the content of the dimensions they used. An evaluative component was more obvious among members of the right-wing groups, with concepts of power and control especially relevant to them.

Rokeach's analysis of rigidity and conservatism (1960), and Eysenck's analysis of social attitudes also reflect the bipolarity there is in emotional and cognitive styles. Comrey (1966), using both personality and social-attitude measures, found nine personality and three attitude factors, which he combined to three second-order factors of conservatism, social desirability and neuroticism, the latter being personality factors. In this study, conservatism accounted for 40 per cent of the variance.

The expressions of conservatism are obviously defined by some content which is itself influenced by cultural and historical factors. Rigidity, tough-mindedness, defensiveness and similar terms refer to more general modes. Attitudes to ethnic groups can reflect hostility, authoritarianism may involve acquiescence, and attitudes to mental health may reflect judgements about undesirable traits.

Organizational ideologies. The attitudes and motives for social control have been well identified. Some rest on coercion, fear and direct control over behaviour, and others on subtle (ideological) appeals to persuade or coerce. These have been translated into theories about organizational goals and about appropriate forms of managerial behaviour; so McGregor (1960) has advanced a Theory X and a Theory Y of management. Theory X is the traditional view that because people dislike work they must be coerced, controlled, directed and threatened before they will work. Theory Y holds that work is as natural as play and rest, and that individual or organizational goals can be integrated.

Whyte has described the growth of an ideology which defines processes that bind men as parts of large organizations, and who then talk of their work in the treadmill or the rat race and of their inability to control their own fate. A common work ethic is derived from the Protestant Ethic, which became the 'American Dream' that 'pursuit of individual salvation through hard work, thrift, and competitive struggle is the heart of the American achievement' (1956, p. 4). This can be replaced by a social ethic 'which makes morally legitimate the pressures of society against the individual' with three major propositions: a belief in the group as the source of creativity, a belief in 'belongingness' as the ultimate need of the individual, and a belief in the application of science to achieve the belongingness (p. 7).

Other formulations and restatements of attitudes to work are elaborated in Whyte's book, where some accounts of the processes of indoctrination into organizational life are also given. Whyte has found support for his views in the increased numbers of business majors and in the numbers of people who are subjected to personality testing, of which he says 'criticism has served mainly to make organizations more adept in sugar-coating their purpose' (p. 9). One way in which the organizational ideology operates can be found in the implicit criteria used for selection. So Whyte sets out the ideals of the 'new model executive' (p. 129), and in an Appendix, 'How to Cheat on Personality', he gives the following advice:

Repeat to yourself: (a) I loved my father and my mother, but my father a little bit more, (b) I like things pretty well the way they are, (c) I never worry much about anything, (d) I don't care for books or music much, (e) I love my wife and children, (f) I don't let them get in the way of company work.

He proceeds to other advice, like 'Stay in character', 'Be emphatic to the values of the test maker', and 'Incline to conservatism'. The reaction against psychological testing has caused many protests against its widespread use, and against similar invasion of privacy (e.g. Conrad, 1967); photos of pickets outside the APA Headquarters in Washington can be found in the *American Psychologist* for November 1965, (vol. 29, pp. 871–2). Chinese psychologists are reported to condemn intelligence testing as capitalistic (Chin and Chin, 1969, p. 194), and 'the anti-test revolt' has been described in Gross (1962).

Other techniques can be used to pursue ideologically defined ends in organizations, and criticism of them is recurrent.

Robinson *et al.* (1969) reviewed seventy-seven scales that relate to occupational attitudes and occupational characteristics, especially to job satisfaction. These have been criticized on ideological and political grounds since a psychologist in industry seems to be aligned either with management or workers, and it is probably impossible to work in the interests of both at once. Kimmel (1969) has traced the conditions that influenced research on work and the worker in the US and he notes that this research began systematically around 1910. Mayo's Hawthorne studies were a later milestone (Rothlisberger and Dickson, 1939) and involved social-psychological skills as well as the skills of the engineer. This work becomes ideologically interesting when the methods used to validate occupational attitudes are examined. The criteria have included measures of productivity or labour turnover, absenteeism or job performance, and vague states of positive 'satisfaction'. Yet for too many of the work scales that Robinson *et al.* review, they note that 'no validity data are reported'.

The validity of any attitude scale is usually assessed by predicting an external criterion, although Scott (1968, p. 252) argues that the instances where some simple criterion of validity is applicable are rare. The use of known groups for validation may be inappropriate because of the opportunistic way that selection into these groups takes place. Any validation is a slow, difficult process, in which both construct and convergent approaches are needed, while the construct that is to be measured must be initially well defined.

National ideologies. National ideologies can be assessed and the early work on national character was full of ideological material, even if not explicitly so. Taft's Australianism scale in which judgements of approval or agreement are to be made about typical Australian social values is a more recent example. The items include wine drinking, food preference, the use of a foreign language in public, and the rights of parents in their old age to be looked after by their children. The scale has been used in several studies of migrant assimilation to define ideas about culturally accepted forms of behaviour. Recent evidence suggests that some Australian norms are changing towards 'European opinions' and that this particular set of items is losing its strength (cf. Jaunzems and Brown, 1972). The fact remains that assimilation to a new culture involves ideas and opinions about what will be involved, as well as some evaluation of the new patterns of attitude and behaviour that are required (cf. Taft, 1965).

The kibbutz ideology is another form of national ideology. Arien (1967) identifies it as 'a hybrid of socialist and Zionist principles'. He extracted ten elements of this ideology from relevant literature and formulated attitude items for them. The items were expressed in behavioural and ideological terms, so the principle that 'Those Jews in the diaspora who are at the summit of the economic pyramid must form its base in Israel' was expressed as, 'If you were an experienced professional in the diaspora, would you be willing to immigrate to Israel even if it meant working at physical labour?' In addition, the subjects were asked to estimate 'the proportion of the population which might agree with the element (public acceptance) or the contribution the ideological element is making to Israel's development (utility).' The following elements or principles were included:

1. Complete mutual responsibility according to the principle 'From each according to his ability, to each according to his needs.'
2. The establishment of society without any differences in privilege or material possession.
3. The abolition of the private ownership of the means of production.
4. Society gives man his character and society stands above the individual.
5. The image of the Jews in Israel must be that of a labouring nation.
6. The realization of the principles of the kibbutz ideology must take place within an agricultural framework.
7. The Jews of the world constitute a nation and not only a religion.

8. General immigration of all Jews to Israel.
9. Those Jews in the diaspora who are at the summit of the economic pyramid must form its base in Israel.
10. Kibbutz values should be accepted as the values of all mankind.

The main aim of the study was to establish empirical inter-relationships between behaviour and 'Idea and Reality', and Arien concludes (with Hegel and against Marx) that 'behaviour is "caused" by Idea and not by Reality', in that 'Ideological commitment "causes" the individual to evaluate reality as he does' and leads to 'behaviour and perceptions of reality consistent with the tenets of the ideology'.

Cultures involve a series of ideologies, and one of the impediments to assimilation into a culture may depend on the unacceptability of these ideals. Taft's concept of secondary integration applies here but, beyond the processes that facilitate identification, there are other ideological factors operating. Thus Taft describes satisfied immigrants as puritan and conservative in their work ethic (1965, p. 44). A good fit between an individual migrant's aims and the social expectations imposed on him will facilitate his assimilation, and some initial willingness to change may facilitate assimilation.

Other ideologies: other methods. The listing of ideologies could go on, but enough illustrations have been given. Omissions include the youth culture, counter cultures, morality and sex ethics. Volumes of the *Journal of Social Issues* take up some of them: vol. 23, 1967, is devoted to family planning and to student activism. The classical sources include views about man and the human condition, like Rousseau's noble savage corrupted by science and reason, Marx's emphasis on classes and property and Freud's socially constrained man. Conceptions about people are an important focus for ideologies. The social scientists' view of man as a behaving organism has been rejected by some because it has led to dehumanization, and obscures the ways in which society's goals are in fact mediated by individuals (Ingleby, 1970). Ideologies are now very commonly identified, and the search for them becomes a game. So male–female differences assume an ideological significance. Apart from descriptions of the need for the liberation of women (Greer, 1971), there are many recognized personality measures, like Terman's masculinity–femininity test and the Mf scale of the MMPI[1], which involve interests and expressed preferences for jobs related to defined sex roles. Such personality measures have been validated against samples of men and women and the result is a reflection of the polarity of sex-related behaviours into which people are forced. The contemporary movement for women's liberation shows the possibilities for change when ideologies are identified and accentuated.

Ideologies can perhaps be most clearly distinguished in an alien system. Chin and Chin (1969) have described the post-revolutionary 'development of ideas in psychology in Communist China and their relation to the socio-political scene' (p. 8). They note about this psychological system that 'The fate of psychology must be studied as a fluctuating process of adjustment between ideological pressure and political movements on the one hand, and methodology and the maturation of ideas on the other' (p.1). The basic Chinese model was imported from the Soviet Union and had a philosophical base in Marx's dialectical materialism with 'Pavlovianism' added. The 'reformed' psychology left 'reactionary' ideas, and used class as the only correct stand-point (p. 211). Thus the psychological justification for the extensive memorization of Mao's sayings 'reflects the primacy of ideas, the stimulation of the active consciousness and the emulation of the hero of heroes' (p. 212). It carries its own special interests; so in medical psychology special emphasis was given to neurasthenia. The Chins note (p. 102) that 'the very choice of neurasthenia as the mass mental health problem for concerted attack was clearly the outgrowth of ideological rather than scientific considerations; for although not much was known medically about neurasthenia, what could be more urgent politically than a relatively widespread but mildly incapacitating ailment that could affect the productivity of a large number of people?'

1. Minnesota Multiphasic Psychological Inventory.

Education, moral character and labour psychology are other special areas, and the Chins conclude that what had emerged by the time of the Cultural Revolution in 1966 'was not a completely politicized psychology . . . but a partially traditional yet Pavlov-based psychology, with particular stress on national control and supremacy of the active consciousness' (p. 39). (See also Gibson, 1972, with Rifkin's criticism that follows it, for a further account of Chinese medical ideology.)

It is possible to identify ideologies underlying punishment, and especially the punishment of criminals. The intention includes retribution and revenge, purification, chastening or admonishing and correction or change through control over positive or negative effects. The fact that prison systems have been operated without clear evidence of their efficacy, and with their high rates of recidivism can be taken as evidence of the difficulties of producing change.

Radzinowicz (1966), in his analysis of the causes and treatment of crime, notes that

The views we hold about why people commit crimes deeply influence our ways of dealing with them. . . . In the period dominated by liberal philosophy, criminals were considered to be otherwise normal human beings, and endowed with virtually unfettered powers of choice and decision. . . . Fundamentally different was the concept which emerged from the doctrines of crime causation, environmental and constitutional, which made so great an impact in the second half of the nineteenth century (determining forces were seen in society or the individual) – and the central issue – dealing with offenders was not to punish their wrong-doing but to secure their more effective control for the future – this was done by considering the nature and circumstances of the offender rather than the offence alone (p. 53).

There are assumed corollaries to any ideology in the jibe that a person 'doesn't have the courage of his convictions', or when people are asked 'what are you going to do about it?' with the implication that overt behaviour should be at least one consequence of an ideology. Most measures relate to an ideology itself and disregard the behavioural components, except perhaps for occasional reference to intentions or to a commitment to disseminate ideas. Some experiments stimulated by dissonance theory about the ways that financial rewards interact with commitment to induce persuasive behaviour could give a paradigm for further studies that might well extend our knowledge of ideology. The behavioural validation of verbal statements of attitude was attempted as an early problem, but it has now largely been discarded with the recognition that attitudes involve evaluative responses, rather than behavioural intentions (Fishbein, 1967). The *knowledge* behind an ideology is also often neglected. But when political attitudes have been interrelated with knowledge about political events, no clear relationships have been found. Similarly there is no direct relationship between religious beliefs and religious knowledge (Hyde, 1965). Most people with strong religious beliefs don't know the ninth Commandment, but of course that knowledge is not often demanded, and if you don't happen to *know* the Commandments you could look them up or find an expert to tell you about them. Yet for those who occupy extreme ideological positions there probably are positive relationships between knowledge and the strength of commitment. Although the consistency theories might seem well suited to analyse these knowledge processes, 'Knowledge' does not appear in the index of either Abelson (1968) or Feldman (1966). The facts that are used to support an ideological position will vary from person to person, as may be seen clearly in the field of religion, while commitment to an ideology may involve a compulsion to make others accept or believe one's own position. There are many difficulties in examining these effects and conformity may be forced by situational constraints.

A further neglected area covers what are construed to be the relevant facts behind sets of ideologies. A little work of this kind has been done for religion, in asking questions like 'What causes you to believe?' (Brown, 1969). Simply plotting the effects of changed knowledge on expressions of attitudes would be a beginning since what passes for evidence itself varies, as do the reasons for coming to adopt an ideological stance. To ask subjects to identify the items in accepted measures like the F-scale or some religious–belief scales might show their sensitivity to ideological material.

Other neglected areas include the ways in which ideologies become shorthand descriptions of complex concepts. It seems to be assumed that people will act for ideological reasons – whether in migrating, participating in protests and revolts, in marrying, or in *not* marrying.

Eysenck (1954, pp. 227–8) refers to a study by Rokeach in which definitions of Buddhism were scored for concreteness. Concrete definitions were more often given by those who were high in ethnocentrism. This may be similar to the difference between narrow and broad categorizing as cognitive styles, and the measures used in those studies could well be adapted to include ideologically relevant material. Sorting tasks could be introduced to explore the recognized content of an ideology. In his study of cognitive tuning, Zajonc extracted scores for complexity, unity and organization from sets of characteristics that subjects themselves listed (1960) and, as we have noted, Scott (1969) developed measures for use in studies of the cognitive structure of nations. Some developments of the methods that allow idiographic material to be effectively summarized might also be applied to ideological material (cf. Bannister and Mair, 1968, chapter 4). In a similar way, Pruyser (1968, p. 80) considers informally some different meanings of 'religion': in the Bible Belt it means praying, Sunday Schools and abstention from various forms of behaviour; and in Harlem it means legal aid, protest marches and mobilizing voters. Systematic extensions of any of these studies could only extend our psychological knowledge.

Recognition and deduction of ideologies over a variety of contexts might provide information about their accessibility and application. Descriptions of behaviour of known value, like engaging in a protest against a visit by the head of a foreign state or protesting about a sporting or cultural exchange, could be set up and questions asked about the underlying ideas assumed to be involved.

There are congruities (and incongruities) between groups and between issues. If these were all to be systematically explored, they might show something of the breadth of ideological positions and the ways they are structured. Subjects could be asked to elaborate ideologies, like 'a Catholic view of divorce', 'a Marxist view of divorce', 'a Labour view of abortion', in a way similar to Triandis and Triandis's (1962) technique that was used to define the links between personal characteristics in racial prejudice. Their content was rated on semantic scales. Alternatively, arguments to justify opening shops for twenty-four hours a day, or for or against abortion, might be analysed for their ideological content.

Psychologists may have been too ready to move away from the detailed specification of ideas and from the content embodied in opinions, because forced-choice methods provided easily handled data that fitted into traditional stimulus-response models of the organism. But the beliefs of *individuals* must be carefully studied before trends across groups can be interpreted, and systematic content analysis gives better information than can the casual introspection or observation that has often preceded the construction of a new scale.

4 Experimentally Studied

It is well recognized that to interpret intercorrelations between sets of measures allows weaker conclusions than does an experimental intervention in which a variable is systematically manipulated, and its effects on other, dependent measures observed. The strength of adherence to an ideological position and the actual content of beliefs have both been used as variables in experiments. Dependent effects have been measured through conventional tests, in the outcome of experimental games or by measures of other responses that have some theoretical significance. Progress in understanding these effects rests on our being able to make precise measures, and on some convergence in the findings of separate studies. One difficulty has arisen from the constant tendency to *explain* ideologies and to treat them as dependent variables themselves, stemming from prior factors like social class, social influence, education, personality, or other less tangible effects that may influence the choice or the strength of an ideology. Too much work in this field is still essentially descriptive, and the effects of ideologies on other psychological and social variables need to be studied in their turn.

We can do no more here than indicate the nature of experimental approaches to ideology. Detailed reviews like McGuire's (1968 and 1969) accounts of attitude change, or a general text like Jones and Gerard (1967) show the breadth of work that has been carried out in experimental social psychology. Reference to these reviews also shows the enormous literature that is relevant to questions about the ways in which ideologies as existing states of belief or attitude interact with communications that are directed at making specific changes. Also relevant are the studies of group functioning that have used ideological and related states as variables (e.g. Dittes and Kelley, 1956; Charters and Newcomb, 1958).

Experimental social psychology has had its main impact on the study of group behaviour and on tests of the balance, consistency and congruity theories of attitudes. These studies vary in the complexities of their design, and in the degree to which some deception is necessary to bring the variables under control. In fact a distinction can be made between studies in which experimental control is achieved through deception or by role playing, thus realizing the ideal of a random allocation of subjects to treatments, and those studies in which the subjects' own states of belief are assessed, and manipulation of the independent variable is through a deliberate selection or allocation of subjects.

Central to any experiment is the fact that the experimenter controls an independent variable in a known and specified way, and holds constant, or in some other way eliminates, the effects of the extraneous variables in which he has no interest, but which might influence the outcome of the experiment. The factors that are not of direct interest are randomized or eliminated by selecting the subjects for the experiment from those who are homogeneous with respect to the defined variables. Without such control, any effects on the dependent variable might be confounded by unknown, or at least by unpredicted, effects of extraneous variables interacting with the independent variable the control of which was the object of the experimental manipulation. Commonsense suggests that in experimental studies of ideology extraneous factors to be controlled should at least include sex, age and probably education.

Interpreting results

Experiments are therefore designed to show any clear-cut effects that may exist. Aronson and Carlsmith (1968) discuss some of the difficulties and problems that are encountered in designing social psychological experiments. The need for complete control is fairly obvious, as use of the experimental method rests on the fact that control of variables and manipulating only one (or more of them) at a time produces controlled effects on the dependent variables. Appropriate statistical tests applied to the results allow estimates of the confidence with which any systematic changes in the dependent variable can be attributed to the experimental manipulations. Interpretation of the results of an experiment may itself be influenced by extraneous ideological considerations. Difficulties of interpretation because of uncontrolled confounding variables are well illustrated by the observations and the experiments which have shown links between smoking and lung cancer. The early observations on which this conclusion (or hypothesis) was based were epidemiological and correlational, as in fact many initial observations must be. Interest in these observations led to more systematic studies that contrasted defined groups, and to the inclusion of questions about smoking in many other inquiries. The amount of smoking therefore defined an independent variable and the incidence of lung cancer became a dependent variable. Various interpretations of the results of these studies have been advanced, and those (like R. A. Fisher) who argued against the casual nature of the relationship between smoking and lung cancer were attacked on the grounds that they had some other commitment (for example, to the tobacco companies) which biased their judgement of the results. Individuals who smoke must also resolve the evidence for themselves so that they can continue smoking, or they will give it up (Borgatta and Evans, 1968). Some claim that there is uncertainty in the interpretation of these results because smoking as an independent variable is confounded with extraneous variables, including personality traits like extraversion (Eysenck, 1965). A more obviously ideological dispute was the Lysenko controversy over the inheritance of acquired characteristics (Graham, 1972, chapter 6). Within contemporary psychology, arguments about the genetic or social basis of observed differences in measured intelligence have developed an ideological flavour, especially when the arguments are applied to the intellectual characteristics of the Blacks in America. The positions adopted by some of the contestants in this dispute even look as if they are politically motivated. This applies to the stance of the extreme environmentalists as much as to that of the hereditarians. Causal links can only be established with certainty by a deliberate and controlled manipulation of variables and by randomly allocating subjects to groups, as for example, to smoking and non-smoking conditions or treatments. But random allocation is impossible with many of the variables in which psychologists are interested.

Experimental intervention

For good studies of ideology one must have a valid measure on which to base the selection of subjects. There is a circularity here since observed or hypothesized differences on some dependent measure give evidence about the validity of the measures that are used to differentiate or identify groups. Although the development of most psychological tests, including intelligence tests, has often rested on a validation against known groups, the purists (another group of ideologists?) reject as 'experiments' those procedures in which scores of groups or individuals are used to define an independent variable. When tests are used, subjects with scores in the top and bottom quartiles of a distribution are usually contrasted, and so the subjects are not randomly assigned to treatment groups, but are selected on the basis of their prior characteristics. Any comparison of high and low scorers is to Aronson and Carlsmith just another use of a correlational method (1968, p. 40). They argue for more complete control, and for experiments in which the experimenter manipulates all the conditions. An experimenter would, for example, give his subjects a false feedback of their attitude scores, and in this way determine who will receive which scores.

Numerous experiments in social psychology have involved systematic deception in an attempt to allocate subjects randomly to conditions, and this has been a matter of controversy. Other approximate forms of control have been tried; one common technique has involved role-playing, or giving an instruction like, 'Complete the following: "For me, becoming a Catholic would mean . . ."', after a counter-attitudinal essay had been written (Brock, 1962).

Although primarily used to explore questions of organization or structure, the modification of belief systems under hypnosis is a further example of experimental control (Rokeach, 1969; Stachowiek and Moss, 1965). Rosenberg (1960) used a similar method to examine experimentally the effects of induced inconsistencies in a set of integrated beliefs – specifically about a carpet salesman who liked modern paintings in his showroom although the paintings drove away his customers. Some debriefing is often used to assess the effectiveness of experimental manipulations, unless one is to believe that all experimental results are in any case due to demand characteristics, to the norms of self-representation or to experimenter expectancy. But hopefully, even these biases could be controlled.

Actual procedures must be settled by the requirements of a particular experiment, but Aronson and Carlsmith also argue that an independent variable must be a condition to which the subject reacts, and cannot be an organismic variable. It seems clear that ideologies are commonly organismic variables, being an existing characteristic of the subjects studied in any experiment, and prior selection is necessary whenever an organismic variable is involved. All the relatively stable psychological characteristics are organismic variables, as are most sociological characteristics. An alternative to contrasting subjects with specified scores on a test is not to use selected subjects but to intercorrelate the scores from several measures, usually across different groups of subjects. The results of that procedure will be considered later (see page 151). Experimental and correlational procedures both have a place: the latter are better for describing groups and an experimental procedure is necessary for the systematic examination of defined effects.

In experimental studies of ideology, the independent variable is specified either by scores on recognized or specifically designed tests or by using labels to denote an ideological position. These labels include political affiliation (Communist, Republican or Labour) and religious identification (Catholic or Jew). Independent variables can be defined relatively easily in these ways, provided appropriate samples are available. Definitions of the dependent variable often derive from the hypothesized relationships, which in turn rest on the theory being tested. Some theories and concepts may not translate well into measurable variables and there is always the possibility that an independent variable will not show any effects on the dependent variable selected. Cunning and shrewdness are needed in formulating theories and in specifying the dependent measures that are to be used. Dependent measures should always be valid and reliable, especially when they are based on ratings of performance or of verbal content.

Dependent variables

Some experiments have used questionnaires to assess the dependent variables, or performance on cognitive or personality-psychological tests. The analysis of this material may use either the content of the replies or structural characteristics like certainty, regardless of content. Other measures include responses that are not under voluntary control and so (in principle) are removed from deliberate bias. The use of pupil size (Woodmansee, 1970) and GSR[1] (Dawson, 1969) are examples. Dawson adopted the traditional–modern dimension of attitudes as a key to explore some beliefs among 'primitive' groups in contact with, and in transition to, modern, Western forms. He reports that GSR responsiveness to relevant concepts was greatest among his Chinese subjects who had not resolved a conflict between the traditional and modern modes. Other response measures include measures of accuracy on a task, the latency of making a decision or choice between alternatives, the speed or rate of response, and the length of time spent looking at alternatives (Jones and Gerard, 1967, p. 195). Such measures require that the subject is given an instruction about the kind of response to be made, and assume that the independent variable has facilitating effects on these responses.

Several programmes of research have made substantial contributions to an understanding of social psychological processes. The cumulative nature of these research efforts is as important as is their essentially experimental formulations. The work of Hovland, of Festinger and of Newcomb are ready examples. The groups that have contributed most to

1. Galvanic Skin Response.

experimental studies of ideology have been centred on Christie at Columbia, on Rokeach at Michigan State and in the earlier Californian studies of the *Authoritarian Personality* (Adorno *et al.*, 1950). Each of these groups began by constructing measures bound closely to a defined theory, and then, partly as a means of validation, used these measures to define an independent variable from which to assess the effects of other dependent measures.

Some experiments

Hypotheses about the effects of ideologies relate to either social-psychological or intrapersonal and personality-based variables. As an analogy to ideological differences, consider the nature of social class. Class cannot be used as a dependent variable but it has been used as an independent variable and has been found to influence psychological variables like judgements of the size of valued stimuli (cf. Bruner and Goodman, 1947; Bruner and Postman, 1948), and conceptually based judgements (Warren, 1966). The selectivity of perceptual and related responses are undoubted effects of central directive states, and these could include accepted ideologies and values (cf. Dixon, 1971, chapter 10). Whether social class differences can themselves be construed as ideological or are only involved with social identity is not to be considered here. But a particular social class position implies some consistency of belief about questions beyond the class structure itself, and can have effects on behaviour.

Warr and Knapper have discussed studies showing that political beliefs influence judgements about, and conceptions of British politicians (1968, p. 97 and *passim*). They report an experiment in which Anglicans responded to (or perceived) an Anglican stimulus more positively than a Catholic stimulus, while Catholic judges perceived a Catholic stimulus more positively than an Anglican stimulus. In this experiment the stimulus was a statement that purported to be the opinions, attitudes and stance of a Church official, and judgements about him were made on a series of semantic differential scales. The dependent response measures were obtained from these semantic rating scales.

Christie and Geis's book, *Studies in Machiavellianism* (1970), relates to a measure of interpersonal manipulation. This work derives from Christie's criticisms of the *Authoritarian Personality* (see page 49), and is a model of its kind. It also shows the diversity of dependent measures that could be used or considered in studies of ideology. After discussing correlations between Machiavellianism and other measures, it was concluded that the only significant relationships were with measures of cynicism and hostility, and (negatively) with social desirability.

In chapter 4 of Christie and Geis, Exline and his group describe an experiment in which each of twenty-four male and twenty-four female subjects worked with another subject on a series of ten decision tasks that required discussion to reach a solution. In each dyad, one member was a confederate of the experimenter, and the subjects were counterbalanced with respect to sex across experimenters, and with respect both to scores on the Mach IV scale and the conditions under which later accusations of cheating were to be made. The primary dependent variable was the duration and direction of gaze between the subject and the experimenter throughout the interaction, but particularly when cheating was being discussed. After a base-line had been established in each group, the decision tasks were introduced in a series of increasing difficulty. When the sixth problem had been presented, the experimenter was called from the room and the confederate subject began to cheat and look up answers to the remaining problems in the experimenter's papers. Motivation for success was arranged by promising $10 for the best group overall. When the series of ten problems had been completed, the subjects were interrogated either together or singly (depending upon the condition) and then accused of the cheating in which they had all become implicated. It was hypothesized that high Machs would use eye contact as a strategy to conceal their cheating more often than would the low Machs. The data supported this hypothesis. High Machs reduced their looking time only 9·5 sec/min after being implicated in the cheating, while the low Machs 'looked away considerably more – some 14 sec/min' (p. 66). High and low Machs were also compared on a number of other dependent measures, including the mean length of mutual glance, number of confessions of cheating elicited, resistance to being involved in cheating and their denial of cheating. The high Machs were found to put up a greater resistance to attempts to implicate them in cheating, and lied more plausibly (as rated by independent judges) after having been accused.

This simplified account of a rather complex experiment illustrates the nature of experimental manipulations when plausible effects are needed to produce an effect on other variables. Christie and Geis describe other experiments that involved interaction, bargaining for rewards, experimental games like the Prisoner's Dilemma (in which each player makes independent choices to achieve a joint outcome) and a 'ball and spiral' game, which involved cooperation to move the ball. In all these experiments the independent variable was controlled by a prior classification of the subjects. High Machs were found to differ from low Machs in their performance on these dependent tasks. They were also found to be better able to learn the subtle cues to be responded to in judging photos of the successful contestants in a brewery's annual beauty competition. Altogether the results of fifty experimental situations are summarized (pp. 290–93) and the high Machs consistently manipulate more, win more, are persuaded less, persuade others more, and in general differ from low Machs as predicted in these situations in which subjects interact face to face with others, and when the 'situation provides latitude for improvisation and the subject must initiate responses as he can or will, and in situations in which affective involvement with details irrelevant to winning distracts low Machs' (p. 312). It should be emphasized that all these results relate consistently to an ideology, or predisposition, about interpersonal manipulation.

Perceptual effects

Rokeach reports correlational data and a number of experiments that were designed to validate his measures and his theory about the ability of those with open or closed cognitive systems to cope with new cognitive material. In one experiment (1960, chapter 14) subjects who were extremely high or low on the Dogmatism Scale were selected and tested individually on several perceptual tasks; first on the Gottschaldt embedded-figures test, which involves finding a given simple figure embedded in a more complex design, and then on an adaptation of Koh's block-design test in which red and white patterns were first to be reproduced with four blocks and later in an enlarged form, with nine blocks and rotated through 90° with the colours reversed. Little difference was found between the open- and closed-minded groups on the perceptual *analysis* involved in the embedded figures test. There were, however, some differences between the groups in the speed with which they *synthesized* the 'new' block designs, although the differences were less for the first two items than for the remaining four items (and these differences only approach the 0·05 level) (p. 265). Although not strong effects, they are consistent. In other experiments, subjects high and low in dogmatism judged samples of 'conventional' and unconventional music (Brahms and Schonberg respectively), or told TAT[1] stories that were later scored for their use of past, present and future tenses. The open-minded group gave more present tense responses and the closed-minded group used the future tense most often (p. 369). The effects that Rokeach has examined systematically are primarily cognitive, and consistent with his theory that dogmatic, bigoted persons exhibit a general trait of concrete and narrow cognitive functioning.

One of the criticisms of the study of *The Authoritarian Personality* was the extent to which the ratings of the variables in the original study were contaminated, and that no account was given of procedures to protect against biases, especially when rating answers to the projective questions. Frenkel-Brunswick (in Christie and Jahoda, 1954) described some cognitive patterns associated with authoritarianism as well as a 'unity of style' that was explored 'through experimentation on perception and thinking', as a deliberate move away from emotional variables to perceptual measures to control such

1. Thematic Apperception Test.

biases. In a brief summary, she notes that a 'tendency to resort to black–white solutions, to arrive at premature closure – often at the neglect of reality – and to seek for unqualified and unambiguous solutions which had been found so characteristic of the social and emotional outlook of ethnocentric subjects could also be ascertained in their perceptual responses' (1954, p. 245). The concept of 'intolerance of ambiguity' has become a common description of this perceptual style. Eysenck discussed similar effects on other measures of perceptual and cognitive rigidity, including Rokeach's 'water jug problems', in relation to ethnocentrism, and to his measure of tough-mindedness (1954, p. 226). These experiments have all rested on a theory about a general style of response. In other experiments some particular content has been examined, as when the ideological state of the subjects is used as the independent variable in studies of the accuracy with which conclusions are drawn from syllogisms (e.g. Thistlethwaite, 1950; Feather, 1964).

Negotiation

Recent studies of negotiation between pairs of subjects, usually in an experimental game where independent choices result in a joint or interdependent outcome for both participants, have revealed the common strategies that develop. The consistent behaviour that emerges is commonly labelled 'competitive' or 'cooperative'. Kelley and Stabelski (1970) conclude from a review of studies that used the Prisoner's Dilemma that 'cooperators will believe others are heterogeneous as to their cooperativeness versus competitiveness, whereas competitors will believe other persons are uniformly competitive', and that 'evidence relating to authoritarianism is found to conform to the same paradigm', in that 'low authoritarians tend to behave like cooperators in experimental game situations and to have beliefs about other persons similar to the cooperators' beliefs'. Their broad conclusion is that a personality disposition influences social behaviour to determine the information that is gained from the social environment and the beliefs that are held about it. Ideologies might well be found to have comparable effects.

As an example of an experiment in which cooperative behaviour is used as a dependent variable, Lutzker (1960) selected subjects on the basis of their scores on a measure of internationalism. It was found that in the Prisoner's Dilemma the internationalists were *not* more cooperative than a control group, but that they were more persistent in seeking cooperation. Isolationists were significantly less cooperative and more competitive than either the internationalists or the control group. Internationalism was defined as trusting other nations and believing that international tensions are reducible by mediation. Some of the items used to measure internationalism were taken from Adorno *et al.* (1950), others were rather general, like 'There will always be wars because, for one thing, there will always be races who try to grab more than their share.' Some items related to specific issues, like 'All military training should be abolished.' In another study, McClintock *et al.* (1963) reported significant differences in the cooperative choices of those high and low on internationalism. Competitive and cooperative behaviour, therefore, bears a dependent relationship to expressed ideologies of internationalism and authoritarianism.

5 Acquired through Learning

Study of the attitudes and ideologies of children has been relatively neglected, except for the work on politics and religion, yet the acquisition of attitudes is one end-product of socialization. It is obvious that attitudes and beliefs are learned, whether explicitly by assimilation from the social environment or generalized from specific experiences. This very common-sense solution to questions about the learning of attitudes leaves aside other psychological questions about any underlying conditions that may facilitate this learning or may predispose to some kinds of attitudes rather than to others. But a continuing line of theory has stressed the relationships between attitudes and the personality processes that develop during childhood. This argument is more commonly used to explain the style of a person's attitudes than the actual content, since specific attitudes can be attributed to the predispositions set up in general response styles.

The critical importance of a child's social environment does not need documentation. Children easily echo the attitudes and the beliefs that they are offered by their peers and by adults. Adults also teach implicitly by reinforcing or punishing certain kinds of responses, and by their specific advice about how this social group should be treated, and how to act or what to believe about that issue. A child will also generate some idiosyncratic beliefs, misbeliefs and attitudes for himself. The contexts of social influence therefore set up critical models for learning. Whether the child learns to respond imitatively, or learns to fulfil social roles and to recognize norms of behaviour, he is not just a passive learner as he must be reactive to his environment. His reactivity may be cognitive and based on understanding, or affective and emotional. In general all children move from being under explicit control to having some internalized control in which they anticipate how their responses will be received and in which they also search for, and use new information.

Attitudes thus become integrated and come to direct behaviour. They also supply information and knowledge about the social world. But a child is highly vulnerable to ideological explanations and the formed attitudes of the wider society, with which he may have little direct contact. In fact, it is likely that much of his experience will be formed by expectations that are imposed on him, and which he does not fully understand. We need to distinguish two complementary processes that are working in the socialization of attitudes and beliefs since the external influences and the internal characteristics or responses to these external events interact. The theories that identify these processes may, however, be derived and ideological. So Riegel (1972) has contrasted Anglo-American and European trends in developmental psychology as reflecting capitalistic and mercantile–socialistic orientations respectively. There is an assumption of continuous growth in the first case and 'qualitative growth models' and multiple standards in the other. One interesting aspect of this paper is the fact that it was accepted for publication. There may be an increasing awareness and questioning of the implicit assumptions about developmental processes.

External influences

The contexts of socialization include institutions like family, school and Church that are characterized by their direct influence, the broad social identities of class, ethnicity, culture, and even ideology itself, and characteristics like the intelligence or the temperament of people who are the agents who mediate these influences. The immediate environment interprets and conveys wider influences and sets up recognized norms and roles. So teachers and parents give access to some cultural products and experiences, force certain kinds of behaviour, and at the same time restrict access to others. Sex-typed responses and social prejudices are particularly clear examples of responses that are socially shaped in this way.

Studies of social influence have emphasized the development of character and conscience more than they have stressed any specific knowledge or even the child's own experiences. Yet it is within his family that a child learns to cope with adults, and his sibling position will influence his experiences and the responses that he can make. At school he meets a wider social environment. Ideas about what are the critical social experiences have changed. Early work and advice tended to be dominated by Freudian theory and stressed control over the basic drives like sex and aggression. Recent work has stressed social control and the rules a child must learn if he is to survive socially. Some of these changes can be traced through alterations in the advice that parents are given about the proper forms of child-rearing. This has potent effects on forms of discipline and on the values inculcated. Wolfenstein (1951) has analysed innovations in the ideas of child training given in the US Department of Labor Children's Bureau Bulletins between 1914 and 1945. She is especially concerned with the effects that psychological theories have had in allowing children to play and in a fusion of work and 'fun', with the aim of making work more agreeable, and encouraging parents to enjoy their children.

The family's role in the acquisition of values and behavioural patterns works in three main ways:

1. To transmit valued attitudes and response styles like co-operation or competition. A family's social position whether in class or ethnic terms has itself a profound effect on the attitudes that are presented. The effects of family influences on religious beliefs and on political attitudes during childhood and in later life have often been described (e.g. Hess and Torney, 1967).

2. To give models, set patterns and generally shape up behaviour. Recent work on the forms of language in socialization, or on the consistency with which a child is handled, have shown many subtle effects that influence personality, intelligence and social expectations (Hess and Shipman, 1965).

3. To provide a structure within which behaviour is actually expressed, and in which the number of children, absence of parents, and other structural factors have been shown to determine the patterns of learned behaviour (Goslin, 1969).

These often subtle and always complex matrices of social influence combine to shape responses and are themselves responded to by children, so they provide bases for emotional acceptance or rejection, for obedience and conformity. These may later structure styles that predispose their own consistencies of behaviour.

Changed theories about socialization can well be illustrated by comparing Child's two essays on socialization. In the first (1954) edition of Lindzey's *Handbook of Social Psychology* he emphasized impulses, infant experiences and parental influences on children, and made little reference to the child's own participation in the systems and institutions of society. These institutions are now recognized to be themselves influenced by prevalent social ideologies, and so Zigler and Child in the second edition (1969) of Lindzey and Aronson's *Handbook* stress that theoretical descriptive studies of children's behaviour have broadened our opinions about the importance of these institutional effects. The new emphasis is to be found in Goslin (1969), where external events are shown throughout to impose continuing constraints on the content and effects of socialization.

Some studies

Several methods have been used to collect data about the external influences on behaviour. Usually they have involved inter-relating remembered or reported child-rearing procedures against other dependent measures of behaviour. Too few studies have used longitudinal data from the same children, or even a concurrent observation of parents and their children. Data are typically derived from interviews or questionnaires with parents about their children (Sears, Macoby and Levin, 1957) or from children about their parents (Herbst, 1954). There is no need to describe the detailed findings of these studies. Bronfenbrenner (1958) has discussed their specificity and their occasionally conflicting results, and has criticized the fact that in this work not enough difference is drawn between the mother's actual response to her child and her expectations about the child. Differences between independence and achievement is crucial in a mother's reactions to her child, and may itself be based on some attitudinal or ideological process: thus Bronfenbrenner notes that the mother–child relationship can be based on a developmental or a traditional conception of that relationship. The conception will reflect in the characteristics that are being encouraged in the child. So some mothers are now being influenced by the ideas of the women's liberation movement, which include a rejection of the traditional conceptions of family processes. There are also pronounced differences between social classes (and cultures) in the characteristics that are valued for a mother. Class and ethnic differences in socialization have been well examined in the attempt to identify the effects of ideological differences or simply the consistent personality patterns that occur, with considerable attention to authoritarian responses and achievement orientation.

The studies of authoritarianism (Adorno *et al.* 1950) were precipitated by an interest in the origins of the hostile and ideologically-based expressions of Fascism. From the programme came Levinson and Huffman's (1955) measure of a 'Traditional Family Ideology' (see page 51), which was also used by O'Neill and Levinson (1954) in a study of the factorial structure of authoritarian attitudes. This scale measures attitudes and ideology towards parent–child relationships and child-rearing techniques, to husband–wife roles and relationships, to male–female relationships, and towards values and aims about families in general. A traditional ideology about these effects is related to authoritarian attitudes.

Another family pattern that is relevant to the control of behaviour is the 'Protestant ideology', in which children are typically encouraged to strive to achieve success and independence (McClelland, 1958). It can be seen in the things parents stress in their child-rearing, especially in relation to their value systems and their tolerance of independence training. Pressures to achievement are found implicitly in many social organizations, as in the effects of ability groupings in schools (in Atkinson and Feather, 1966, chapter 15), and other school structures have strong effects on the attitudes and behaviour of their pupils. Dreeben (1967) argues that the characteristic pattern of organizational properties in schools and classrooms is 'different from those of other agencies in which socialization takes place and that what children learn derives as much from the nature of their experiences in the school setting as from what they are taught.' He proceeds to examine the norms (especially of independence and achievement) and the sanctions that operate in schools, and the conflicts that may inhere in them. Himmelweit and Swift (1969) have advanced a model that explores similar problems. In this model the extent to which a child is influenced by school depends on consistent or conflicting values, rewards, sanctions and status within the school. They also give a central place to the school's ideology and tradition in determining its effectiveness.

Once differences between established practices, family structures and patterns are recognized, they must be explained or justified by parents or teachers to themselves, and to their inquiring children. These explanations may be given in some ideological terms, or the patterns may merely be enforced directly and without explanation. This becomes an example of the difference between the elaborated and restricted codes that Bernstein has drawn attention to in the language of child-rearing, but see Coulthard's (1969) criticisms of this work. There may be other discrepancies between the behaviour expected from children and that actually being rewarded or punished.

Institutional effects

Children's ideologies in politics and religion have been quite extensively studied, especially in the search for evidence about an interaction between the child's developing understanding and any specific training that he may be being given. We can take it that developing awareness itself depends on the increased knowledge that results from the training given by parents and teachers. While intellectual development is not simply a maturational process, explicit training stands in contrast to the indirect effects on attitudes and ideologies found for example in the mass media, where perhaps the aim is to indoctrinate. McGuire distinguished education from propaganda so that 'in "educational" situations the independent variable effects attitude change mainly through its relationship to the attention and comprehension mediators, and in "persuasion" situations, mainly via the yielding mediators' (1969, p. 151). Education is assumed to have a rational basis, but even this depends upon one's point of view, since what may be propaganda and indoctrination to one person might be educational and legitimate to another. There are also many implicit influences in any educational process, beyond the effects of the school's social structure, and the actual material being taught. The content of children's reading books, for example, is one way in which cultural, interpersonal and individual attitudes and values are covertly communicated to children. Wiberg and Blom (1970) rated children's reading material from 5 countries on 38 attitudinal sets that covered culture posture, other-directed posture and inner-directed posture. Of their 38 attitudes, 17 discriminated among the countries for the stories they analysed. England and South Korea were found to be high on ambition and initiative, the United States was high on earning, ignorance and intelligence, and West Germany was high on religion. Other systematic differences are to be found in the material used to teach history and geography, and to teach arithmetic. Klineberg (1954, p. 502) refers to the stress on concepts of capitalism in the familiar commercial practices that are used as examples. Better examples might include questions like, 'If in a modern war there were ten million combatants and two million casualties annually, what are the probabilities of remaining unscathed during four years of participation?'

There has been a considerable recent interest in the effects of the mass media on behaviour and ideologies. Lovibond (1967) examined some effects on social attitudes of children reading about crime and violence in comics. His measures involved a modification of the authoritarianism scale, a knowledge of comics test and a test of the effects of exposure to positive moral influences. Lovibond concluded that 'exposure to the media studied influences children in the direction of acceptance of the ideology measured by the Children's F-scale, and exposure to constructive moral influences subtracts from the effects of the media.' Current controversies centre on the continuing effects of violence in films and television and the effects of reading *The Little Red School Book*, which, depending on the reader's stance, merely instructs school children about school, sex, drugs and similar questions, or sets out to encourage revolution and disruption of the school's authority. This *Little Red School Book* by the Danish writers Hansen and Jensen was translated into English, and a New Zealand edition was produced from the British version. That edition of the book was referred to the New Zealand Indecent Publications Tribunal for a decision as to whether it was indecent. In the decision of the Tribunal given on 28 March 1972, the meaning of 'indecent' was traversed, because of the treatment that was given to sex. Of its general educational relevance the Tribunal said

In the eyes of some, it is intended to be totally destructive of the school system and anti-authoritarian and therefore to be banned. In the eyes of others it is intended to be constructive and to improve the school system for all concerned, pupils, teachers and parents.

In fact the hearing swung between these poles, in relation to the 'honesty of purpose of those responsible for the book', and the book was finally classified as 'not indecent'. The hearing illustrates well the feelings that generate around critical issues.

Some studies have contrasted the effects of religious training on moral judgement and behaviour (Wright, 1971) and the effects of exposure to explicitly sexual material. The Report of the US Commission on Obscenity and Pornography concluded from their studies of adults that 'Exposure to erotic stimuli appears to have little or no effect on already established attitudinal concomitants regarding either sexuality or sexual morality' (1970, p. 29). But attitudinal socialization has not yet been well enough explored for us to be able to define all the critical influences. In a study of political socialization, Hess and Torney (1967) found that intelligence was an important factor that limits the acquisition of knowledge about the political system. They examined attitudes that had already been formed and which showed continued effects, rather than a merely transitory misunderstanding. Longitudinal studies that carry forward to adulthood are needed, where changes in beliefs are to be expected and background, intelligence and exposure all limit the comprehension and acceptance of attitudinally relevant material. Goldberg's model (quoted by Sears, 1969, p. 323) 'emphasizes the role of political social-ization in producing durable party loyalties'. The model is shown in Figure 1, and suggests that the vote is 'jointly a product of party identification and partisan attitudes, with the latter also in part a result of the former' (Goldberg, in Sears, 1969, p. 323). The respondent's social background and characteristics only act *through* his party identification or

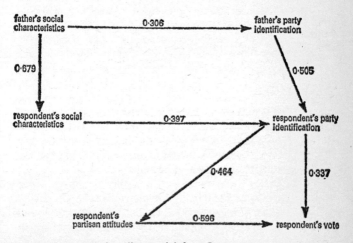

Figure 1 Goldberg's voting model, from Sears, 1969, page 323. 'The numbers are beta weights for the causal relationships specified. Only those significant beyond the 0·01 level are shown'

loyalties. This voting model with its six variables accounts for 50 per cent of the variance in adult voting choice.

Cognitive processes

Any child makes two kinds of response to social influence: one is cognitive and the other is emotional. (There is, of course, the child's actual behaviour too, but this is less important for ideology, which is more concerned with ideas about, or the explanations of, action.)

Piaget has given particular stress to a child's cognitive development and his ability to make abstractions. This links closely with a developing understanding of adult forms of thought. In an early paper entitled 'Children's Philosophies' (1933), Piaget discussed the importance of realism, animism and artificialism as aspects of a child's ideas about himself and the world. Questions like, 'Where does the rain come from?' and 'How did the sun begin?' were asked of children and 'the answers were very uniform and advanced progressively with the age (of the child)'. This progressive development is from thought that uses highly concrete forms to that which is abstract and formal. A young child's beliefs about the world are often mistaken and distorted because of the concreteness of his conclusions. He is later able to make more accurate explanations. Others following Piaget have come to stress the importance of a stimulating educational and social environment in contributing to this development, and especially in developing an ability to decentre and so to take the role of another and to act in a detached way (Flavell, 1968). This process binds together environmental effects and their inner responses and so a child develops personal ideologies or beliefs that he can use to explain his place in his environment.

Ideologies are a necessary part of a child's thought. Oeser and Emery considered that, 'no individual can personally apprehend more than a fraction of the social structure within which he plans to act. Consequently an individual must rely to a considerable extent on social ideologies for an explanation of those aspects of the wider society which may affect his life chances' (1954, p. 48). The method that Oeser and Emery used to assess this development involved counting the number of questions that children left unanswered and the number they said they did not know about, when asked about their knowledge of the adult world. The questions for completion covered four areas and included:

1. There is one country in the world which always wants to start wars. . . .
2. There is one group of people in Australia which always does its best for the rest of us. . . .
3. There are some people in Australia who have all the say in what happens. . . .
4. There are some people in Australia who always get the best jobs. . . .
5. There are some people in Australia who always try to cause strikes. . . .

Since not all children succeeded in answering all of their nine questions, several indices were constructed to show the developing differentiation of beliefs and explanations. From their examination of the pattern of failures to respond to particular questions, Oeser and Emery concluded that some ideological explanations about who causes and who stops events have been absorbed by most children, that they can identify social groups that may further their interest, and have an awareness as to who holds social power. From answers to the questions about jobs they conclude that the specific ideology of success is of great significance with success depending on 'pull', not on personal abilities. They conclude also that anti-communism and prejudice can focus dissatisfaction towards some aspects of the existing society.

Emotional processes

Another set of inner processes is emotionally based. Kagan and Moss (1962) have gathered evidence for some aspects of adult personality beginning to take shape during early childhood. They found however that this continuity is closest when there is congruence with the traditional sex-role characteristics. Passive and dependent behaviour is disapproved for men but not for women, and these forms show the greatest changes with age for men. Direct rewards and punishments are used to bring their expression in line with what is prescribed in the role models (p. 266). Parents obviously differ in the training given, and in doing so they implement their ideas about the appropriate and correct forms of behaviour. This role-related behaviour is a clear example of how an ideology about appropriate behaviour itself forms the behaviour to which it is related. Similar arguments might be applied to fear, security, safety, authority, aggression, cooperation, competition and competence as drives and internal states that come to control and direct an individual's behaviour.

In this material one encounters a continuing controversy that relates to personality theory and developmental study, in the innateness of some behaviour, and the learned nature of traditional adult forms. Kohlberg discussed this controversy (1969, p. 364) and concluded that what he calls the 'motivated traits', like dependence and aggression, are not explained well by inherited terms, although introversion as a trait of style shows continuity and consistency because it does not have a specific content. The greatest developmental changes occur in the cognitive domain because of its reliance on knowledge and understanding (p. 373).

Child-rearing

The distinctions made so far raise questions about the extent to which, or the ways that, the specific content of an ideology can have its influence. Parents as 'child-rearers' use the relatively limited sets of procedures provided by their culture, and which have probably influenced them during their own socialization. This continuity gives great stability to a culture, at least until rapid social change or increased independence takes over and breaks the cycle. But even after a revolution, underlying continuities persevere, as Murvar (1971) argues in his analysis of religious and revolutionary messianism in Russia. Murvar asserts that the non-Russian communist-ruled nations in eastern Europe are implicitly rejecting Russian cultural traditions when they reject Russian political domination.

Inkeles (1955) analysed the value orientations of child-rearing in Russia to compare with the pre- and post-revolutionary periods. He identified six prominent dimensions and says,

The value of 'tradition' was coded mainly for emphasis on religious upbringing, but it included as well references to maintenance of strong family ties and traditions; 'adjustment' reflects emphasis on 'getting along', staying out of trouble, keeping an eye on your security and safety, etc.; 'achievement' was coded when parents stressed attainment, industriousness, mobility, material rewards and similar goals; 'personalistic' was checked when the parent was concerned with such personal qualities as honesty, sincerity, justice and mercy; 'intellectuality', where the emphasis was on learning and knowledge as ends in themselves; and 'political' when the focus was on attitudes, values and beliefs dealing with government and particularly with *the* government of the land.

These are ideologies, and in his results the tradition dimension showed the greatest changes, dropping from 75 per cent to 44 per cent. The emphasis given to material rewards and to tradition declined markedly among the parents who raised their children in the revolutionary era. In the post-Second-World-War period emphasis changed again to seeking jobs assuring self-expression. Changes in values were found to be related to the reasons given for occupational choice. Some of this material is summarized in Table 1.

Table 1 **Changing values in occupational choice**
(from Inkeles, 1955, Table 2)

| | Generation% | |
Value areas	Tsarist	Revolutionary
Rewards	41	25
Tradition	35	14
Self-expression	21	38
Politics	3	23
Number of responses	58	63

This kind of data shows that value changes follow the broad political and other contextual events. One regrets that there has been so little systematic study of these effects: it seems for example that those who grew up in the Thirties may not have given their children economic values that are appropriate for a period of high inflation, and so may have facilitated the 'drop-out' behaviour.

Youth cultures

Havighurst and Keating (1971) have described three recognizable alienated youth groups. There are the hippies, who 'search for a society based on love and whose desire for ecstatic experience has strong religious connotations', and the radical social activists, where much of the leadership has come from young adults connected with religious organizations. Finally there are the uncommitted described by Keniston (1960). There is an enormous literature on the recent phenomena of student *revolt* (Grouch, 1970), student *power* (Cockburn and Blackburn, 1969), student *protest* (McGuigan, 1968) and the young *radicals* (Keniston, 1968). Bay (1970) summarized some of the studies and stressed the need for a functional analysis of the attitudes that are involved. The period of the 1960s has been called a 'decade of protest', and blame for this has been attributed to many factors, including people like Dr Spock, Marx, Freud and Marcuse, and affluence and security as too safe a base for attitudes. Within our present context we can, however, note that those who protest are engaged in social learning experiences, although many have adopted an ideology of alienation or rejection in order to make their protests. But further developmental study is urgently needed to establish how the members of the various groups adapt as they move beyond a period of revolt, of 'developmental estrangement' (Keniston, 1960, p. 475), or through the themes of protest that Flacks (1967) describes in romanticism, anti-authoritarianism, egalitarianism, anti-dogmatism, moral purity, community and anti-institutionalism. These are all ideologies.

Developmental theories

The developmental model applied to the formation of attitudes and values, and so to the formation of ideologies, was dominated at first by a Freudian theory about unconscious structures and the importance of childhood experiences. This gave way to Piaget's theory (1947) in which stress was laid on the development from immature patterns of thought and understanding towards abstract, sophisticated, adult patterns. To put it another way: the Freudian emphasis on impulse-based processes was replaced by attention to the ego-processes, and a recognition of the central role that the demands of social reality impose. These changes may have come about in part because 'structures' like conscience or super-ego came to be studied with behavioural data about the forms of resistance to temptation.

Hess and Torney (1967, pp. 20–21) have identified four models of the child-rearing or developmental process. The first stresses cognitive development and increased understanding. It rests on a recognition of a child's misunderstandings which direct teaching tries to modify. In confrontations between a child and social reality, the child may be excused his 'mistakes' because of immaturity, and the consequences of particular attitudes will not always be accentuated. Whether there will be tolerance must depend on the orientation of the parents, and their child-rearing ideology. Some parents will be rigid in these attitudes, perhaps justifying them on political or religious grounds. The second model identified by Hess and Torney they call 'the accumulation model'. It is the least psychological since it assumes a didactic training which the child must accept. A lot of formal teaching rests on the belief that education and training can be delivered and directly absorbed. The third model uses the concept of identification with some elements of imitation, and the fourth is an 'interpersonal transfer model' in which role-appropriate behaviour is generalized from the specific cases that are presented to a child. These processes may work simultaneously, but have greater effects on some kinds of information or material than on others.

Development generally moves towards abstraction, and perhaps to the recognition of some ideological content. But what is it that facilitates the recognition of ideological content? We can recognize that a child becomes aware of the way in which society uses labels that imply differences in belief and behaviour. Elkind (1963) studied the development of religious identity, using Piaget's method of a semi-clinical interview. He found in the first stage that children had a global undifferentiated conception of their denomination, and that in the second stage (usually around age 7–9) their conception became concrete in the sense that observable features or actions were invoked to make the definition. Thus a Jew is one who goes to Temple, while a Catholic goes to Mass. At the third stage the conception of denomination becomes abstract and differentiated, and expressed usually in terms of belief and understanding. This development runs parallel with the well-documented changes in intellectual understanding towards the stage of formal operations.

A child abstracts values from behaviour and so honesty, loyalty and similar ideas become integrated into the self-concept. A young child is essentially a realist and only later does he develop into an idealist: the conflicts between some ideal, abstract world and social reality may themselves cause the crises of adolescence that were once regarded as a peculiar characteristic of this period of development (cf. G. S. Hall in 1902). But the necessary breakdown of realism can be seen in the changes that take place in the forms of acceptance and the content of religious belief and attitude. These changes have been well studied through conceptions of God, in which the progress is always towards greater abstractness (e.g. Graebner, 1964).

An important task for a child is to understand and come to terms with his environment. A major source of variation in this development derives from the complexity, the directedness and the responsiveness to environmental change of the child's cognitive structures, although the socializing agents who interpret the adult environment and administer and control the reinforcements of behaviour are also critical. In the development of political and religious ideologies, while the school and the family will both give direct teaching, much of their influence is still indirect. So political attitudes may, for example, show the influence of attitudes towards authority and rules, with compliance generally transformed and applied. The patterns of adult voting behaviour may be much less important in general political terms than are the subtle effects of these basic behavioural patterns. So children learn their attitudes in different social contexts, each of which may itself be ideologically controlled.

6 Explained in Social Terms

Some say that ideological differences reflect struggles between groups or classes, with psychological, behavioural or personal factors secondary to the economic or other principles involved. Others say that ideological differences reflect struggles between individuals fighting for power or seeking to resist those already in power. Both of these interpretations involve social-psychological processes that influence the behaviour of actors who are ideologically involved, perhaps because the mere presence of others has positive effects on behaviour (Zajonc, 1968). So group influence and support maintains ideologies as socially relevant, and defines specific beliefs and attitudes.

Membership in a social group provides an important personal reference system. It is also an important source of information for an individual. When a group embodies or makes available an ideology, the ideology can itself contribute to social cohesion and may legitimize social categories and relationships. Identification as a 'worker', as 'coloured', as a 'woman' or a 'friend', can accentuate social differentiations that may have previously been implicit or unacknowledged. Consider as an analogy the experiment of Brown and Lenneberg (1954) which showed that while there are more discriminable colours than there are colour names, an available vocabulary for colours influences the separate colours that are recognized. Stereotypes and similar labels code our responses to people and to ideas. So individuals become 'tuned' to respond to people as social stimuli. Information about status or expertise, about opinions or affiliations both influence perceptual judgements. An artificial consensus may bias judgements about the length of a line (Asch, 1952) in a way that is rather similar to the ways in which cohesion and conformity restrict the ideas that are accepted by the members of a group. These and other findings have led the various consistency theories to dominate social psychology over recent years. Because of their importance, the concepts and applications of these theories are referred to in several other sections, so that a separate account of them is not needed here.

The social experiences of many people support their ideologies. Distinctions between 'practical' or expedient and 'ideological' reasons do not stop social experiences from being interpreted through an ideology. The interactive or reflexive nature of these effects allows an ideology to bind the thought and judgements of those who accept or recognize it, without their necessarily being aware of the constraints that it imposes, or of the effort needed to preserve some consistency. It is obvious that some will resolve inconsistency by a screening process that limits the experiences to which they are exposed.

Group influences

Charters and Newcomb (1958) considered the ways in which expressed attitudes can be made increasingly similar to those prescribed by the norms of a group in which a person has membership. In their study, groups belonging to the same religious denomination were brought together for a controlled discussion that emphasized the similarities between their beliefs. A seventy-two-item questionnaire was then completed by each subject, and it was found that Catholic subjects expressed attitudes closer to an orthodox Catholic position than did control subjects whose awareness of their group membership had not been stressed in prior discussion. Protestants and Jews did not show the same accentuation because, it was argued, contrary pressures operated against members of these groups showing an awareness of their religious affiliation.

Festinger (1950) examined the way in which knowledge of a person's religious affiliation will influence the behaviour of others towards him. The experimental task in that experiment was to elect 'officers for a club'. Two conditions were run. In one condition religious membership was made explicit and in the other it was not. When the subjects were not religiously identified, Jews and Catholics were found to split their votes equally between other Jews and Catholics. Festinger reported that when the subjects were religiously identified, 'The effect of knowing the name and religion of the other people introduces a considerable change in behaviour. While the Jewish girls still split their votes about evenly between Jews and Catholics, the Catholic girls now give 64 per cent of their votes to Catholics and only 36 per cent to Jews.' In a more rigorous test, paid participants in one group said they were Jews and in another group they said they were Catholics, and almost identical results were produced. Group identity influenced the choices, while the labels probably stand for a detailed ideology.

These experiments show several forces that are at work, including membership and reference effects. The social meaning of both simple and complex stimuli can change when they are put into recognized categories. Cultural and linguistic conventions facilitate this categorization and foster conceptions of the social world that are consistent within groups. Group support always implies some group influence.

The effects of a real social environment on attitudes have been studied by Newcomb. In the Bennington College Study he traced changes in attitudes beyond the direct effects that can be observed in childhood socialization where environmental control is fairly obvious. A university or college environment might be expected to have diverse and varied effects on attitudes. There were three parts to the Bennington Study: Newcomb (1943) first studied the political attitudes of these women students through the years 1935 to 1939, and followed up a majority of them in 1961 and 1964 to establish how stable their political opinions had been. The social norms of the College itself were re-examined in the early 1960s. A principal finding of the first study was that during the years at College most students became increasingly liberal in their attitudes. Interviews showed that the students were rather deliberately choosing this more liberal stance and rejecting the attitudes of their parents. The main reference groups were peers and family, but very few chose to follow their families' patterns. Peer influences were strongly reinforced, helped by the new outlook that the faculty gave to their students. Newcomb *et al.* (1967) later showed that the change away from the family patterns persevered, primarily because the students continued to select reference groups that supported the attitudes they had developed by the time they left college. This was similarly true for the minority who remained conservative. The neat circularity in choosing a group that defines attitudes and later using that group to sustain these attitudes has already been noted.

Other studies of the effects of college have shown its continuing influence on attitudes and beliefs. For example, Feldman and Newcomb (1969) conclude about religion that 'Studies generally show mean changes indicating that seniors, compared with freshmen, are somewhat less orthodox or fundamentalistic in religious orientation, somewhat more sceptical about the existence and influence of a Supreme Being, somewhat less favourable to the Church as an institution' (p. 23). Feldman and Newcomb go on to discuss individual differences in the effects that have been observed, and they stress that different groups will not necessarily show similar amounts of net change so that some individuals show an increase in their religious beliefs. Grouped trends always obscure individual or idiosyncratic effects.

The shaping of attitudes during a professional training, especially in medicine or law, is an example of the explicit control that an educational institution can assume. Conformity to the established norms is rewarded or enforced through all levels of the medical profession which, like any sub-culture, prescribes the ideology that most come to accept although there will still be dissident opinions. It may be hard among those who do conform to distinguish the effects of explicit pressures from an implicit acceptance of the norms.

Recognition of the importance of group influences is not new. Adorno *et al.* (1950) noted that 'Another aspect of the individual's situation which we should expect to affect his ideological receptivity is his membership in social groups – occupational, fraternal, religious and the like. For historical and sociological reasons, such groups favour and promulgate, whether officially or unofficially, different patterns of ideas.

There is reason to believe that individuals, out of their needs to conform and to belong and to believe and through such devices as imitation and conditioning, often take over more or less ready-made the opinions, attitudes and values that are characteristic of the groups in which they have membership' (1950, p. 9). Social influences are inescapable and it is not really necessary to attribute their positive effects to needs and other unconscious processes. A stable social world rests on a consensus, or at least on some effective social control, and it is *resistance* to social influence that might more readily express some personality dispositions.

Many studies have shown that interpersonal attraction is related to congruent belief systems. Deconchy (1968) asked children of known religious affiliation to make sociometric choices within their school class. They were asked about those in their class with whom they would prefer to work on different tasks: strong preferences were found for choices to be reciprocated on the basis of religion.

Social roles

The concept of social role, with its implications for complementarity, expectation and conflict, is said by Sarbin and Allen (1969) to be one that uniquely integrates individuals and society. A social ideology may reinforce and justify social roles by providing acceptable explanations for them. So the subordinate role and status of women is supported by many varied arguments and bits of evidence, as well as by the behaviour of both men and women. Role enactment is also seen in the behaviour of a politician who accepts the constraints placed on him by his party and his supporters. The result is an almost necessary conformity in the expression of approved beliefs (1969, p. 533), while public recognition of a person's stance or set of beliefs increases his commitment to them.

The fact that attitudes become organized around social roles and group membership is well illustrated by Lieberman's study (1956) in which workers elected to positions as shop steward were found to become more pro-union on issues relevant to their new role, while workers promoted to foreman became more pro-management. Within three years the members of these two groups, drawn initially from a homogeneous population, had developed opposing attitudes. When some of these foremen later reverted to jobs on the factory floor, their expressed attitudes altered appropriately.

Attitude change can be forced by outside events. Decisions to admit China to the United Nations, or to have a vernacular Mass, have probably produced some reorganization of many people's attitudes. Any dissonance that is experienced is resolved by one of several available strategies that include rationalizing beliefs or leaving the group. Other changes in public policy have altered behaviour, and have in consequence influenced beliefs and attitudes: repeated surveys have shown that attitudes favourable to school desegregation in the US moved from some 30 per cent in support in 1942, to 49 per cent in 1956 and 62 per cent support in 1963; even in hard-core areas in the South, the extent of approval rose from 4 per cent in 1956 to 28 per cent in 1963 (Sheatsley, 1966).

Social relationships

It is not only attitudes that are influenced by group memberships and social processes. Roger Brown has described the ways in which relationships between people are defined and controlled by conventional forms of address. He studied the use of the pronouns *thou* (T) and *you* (V), which he says express a 'group ideology' about power and solidarity within democratic traditions. His evidence is drawn from several sources. In *The Two Gentlemen of Verona*, for example, Proteus and Valentine 'initially exchange thou, but when they touch on the subject of love, on which they disagree, their address changes to the you of estrangement' (1970, p. 333). Pronouns and other forms can be used to express attitudes. Brown notes that

A strong equalitarian ideology of the sort dominant in America works to suppress every conventional expression of power asymmetry. If the worker becomes conscious of his unreciprocated address to the boss, he may feel that his human dignity requires him to change. However, we do not feel the full power of the ideology until we are in a situation that gives us some claim to receive deferential address. The American professor often feels foolish being given his title, he almost certainly will not claim it as a prerogative (1970, p. 324).

Richardson (1957), reporting on findings from a study of the assimilation of British migrants in Western Australia, noted the importance to migrants of the Australian's vocabulary and usages. Acceptance of new ways of addressing one's boss there is one index of assimilation. So the successful British migrants change their ideas and converge their behaviour to Australia's social norms, perhaps without much clear advice about what the new norms actually are.

Further support for the use of language to indicate one's attitudes about personal relationships is given by Brown (1970) in his study of fifty French students in Boston. They answered Eysenck's social attitude inventory and a questionnaire on the probability of using T or V pronouns with different people including father, mother, grandfather, fellow student, waiter, top boss and army general. The rank-order correlation between scores on Eysenck's measure of radicalism and on the pronoun scale was +0·96. Brown concluded that 'A Frenchman could, with some confidence, infer that a male university student who regularly said T to female fellow students would favour nationalization of industry, free love, trial marriage, the abolition of capital punishment and the weakening of nationalistic and religious loyalties' (1970, p. 329). He says that these linguistic forms express an ideology 'consistent in its disapproval of barriers between people' and break down a separation of the 'solidary, the in-group from the nonsolidary, the out-group' (1970). Social demarcations are expressed in other subtle ways including non-verbal deference (Argyle, 1969, p. 140ff.), and become a major ideological expression in interpersonal behaviour, where what *ought* to be done is important. Any status differences are a direct expression of a social ideology (Sears, 1969, p. 403), and a class structure itself can be assumed to embody an ideology about the nature of society. While the actual terms used may vary from one context or culture to another, some ideologies will circulate that justify differentiation, while other people in the same situation may argue for the breakdown of barriers (cf. Danziger, 1958). There is, however, no necessary consistency here. It is reported that the supporters of Governor Wallace, who advocated the need for law and order, tended to disobey STOP signs (Wrightsman, 1972).

Opinion leaders can be important in producing ideological change, not least through their mediating role. A doctor's decision to prescribe a new drug or a farmer's decision to alter some aspect of his husbandry will be influenced by the available information, and by those he knows who may also change. In a two-step theory of communication it is therefore the leaders who mediate change (Katz, 1957). This has been shown to apply to technological innovations, and probably it also applies to the introduction of ideological changes.

Recognition of an ideology is not necessary before it can have an effect: behaviour without an awareness of social influence is a common finding. So Bem writes of 'training the woman to know her place' as a 'nonconscious' ideology (1970, pp. 89–99). Once an ideology has been identified, the whole basis of the related behaviour can change. Statements about women's liberation or racial or social discrimination can lead to a new perspective on available stimuli and contexts, and so can polarize attitudes or change behaviours. Ideologies seem to be more easily recognized by some who have learned to think in the relevant terms, or by those who are detached from the immediate situation, than by those directly involved. Yet leaders are commonly thought to be controllers of ideologies.

Cultures embody agreed solutions to various problems, and cultural contact gives one way of disseminating ideologies. The effects of cultural differences on future orientation were studied by Gillespie and Allport (1955) when they asked students in several countries to write an autobiography 'From now to 2000 AD and to answer a series of relatively structured questions. Most of the responses were found to be anchored in a basic frame of family reference, with frequent mention of parents and siblings, future families and children, and themes like honesty, reliability, decency and integrity as the values to be imparted to their children. Although these themes were common to all the groups, there were some cultural differences. The American samples valued variety more than did other groups, while the Europeans were more concerned with forming character, and subjects in emergent countries introduced themes of personal achievement and social utility. Stereotypes and concepts about class, religion, race, colour, sex, strangeness, ways of life, values and so on become rallying points for a recognition of the similarities and differences that can be accentuated between groups.

Selective memberships

The nature and purpose of any face-to-face group will determine the selective effects it has on its members, especially when an ideological base is explicitly recognized. Wolfinger *et al.* (1964) sampled the audience of a Christian Anti-Communist Crusade School, run for a week in Oakland, California, by a group of politically conservative white Protestants. They report that more than 75 per cent of those attending were Protestants and only a 'handful' were non-whites. Of the sample drawn, 66 per cent were Republicans and only 8 per cent were Democrats. In these respects the sample was unrepresentative both of Oakland and of the San Francisco Bay area. One of their conclusions is that people expose themselves more to influences with which they agree than to those with which they disagree; probably some direct personal influence initially brings such groups together. The extensive literature stimulated by dissonance theory has shown the common preferences for information that is generally supportive of existing beliefs and behaviour. So Freedman and Sears (1965) in their review emphasize the importance of *de facto* selectivity; 'most audiences for mass communications apparently tend to over-represent persons already sympathetic to the views being propounded, and most persons seem to be exposed disproportionately to communications which support their opinions' (p. 90). Defining these effects completely is rather hard since social utility may lead a person into situations where he finds others who are similar, and with whom he agrees. Disagreements tend to be uncomfortable, and people share experiences more readily with those who hold similar opinions. Selectivity is also facilitated by demographic factors. Freedman and Sears noted that 'large differences in opinion are associated with educational level on a number of issues, such as internationalization, tolerance for ethnic minorities and support for civil liberties'. In each case those holding the more 'liberal' opinions are also more likely to be exposed to any public-affairs material in the mass media by virtue of their greater education. Hence 'liberal' propaganda on these issues is indeed most likely to reach 'liberal' citizens (1965, p. 91). Hudson's (1970b) finding of differences in the initial attitudes, ideas and approaches of students beginning University courses in arts and sciences have already been noted. These opinions are shaped by numerous prior influences.

A distinction must be drawn between the ideologies and the actual contexts of groups in contact or conflict. Many conflicts between groups may be explained on ideological grounds, and while there have been arguments about the extent to which social cohesion rests on reactions to an identified out-group, this interpretation is hard to test. Yet the fact remains that the persecution of individuals, groups or classes has been justified on ideological grounds which may stress what people believe rather than what they do. American attacks on communism give one example of a process that produced demands for public conformity in signing loyalty oaths. But groups differ in the ways they form a consensus, and in their acceptance of rational, independent norms (cf. Sears, 1969, pp. 439–40).

The processes of conformity are important influences on expressions of ideology. The now extensive literature on conformity depends on some observed change in a person's behaviour towards closer agreement with the evident behaviour of other group members. But as Hollander and Willis (1967) suggest, change in behaviour may be the result of many processes, including a deliberate choice, or a simple concurrence of action. In other words, the change may be incidental and not a consequence of group influence. Merely conventional agreement needs to be distinguished from acquiescence that involves a more permanent shift in opinion. Although behavioural conformity can be readily defined, its meaning and the nature of the changes require careful analysis. Hollander and Willis suggest two dimensions of response: independence–dependence and conformity–anticonformity, with the basic or pure modes of responding occurring in conformity, independence and anticonformity. The situational sources of conformity and nonconformity should be predictable from knowledge of the influence sources and from the nature of the situation, but consistency across situations in the behaviour of the same subjects is more difficult to define. Some person-specific behaviours may depend on status, so that high-status people conform 'for internally determined causes while the low-status person is seen to conform for externally determined causes' (1967). In the same way an ideology may not be directly expressed because of situational constraints.

The members of a small group may develop tension and disagreement about the principles that govern their interaction. Within a marriage there are many possibilities for dispute, and these can be accentuated or suppressed, depending on underlying strands of attachment, disaffection, attempted manipulation and so on (Scanzoni, 1968). Compliance to allow some shared reference functions presupposes some form of basic agreement at least about the means of resolving differences. This might be construed as an ideology. Joint action may also conceal ideological and other differences that might emerge in crisis. With differences concealed, interaction can become ritualized or a routine, or may involve peculiar or unique interpretations of the situation.

Disagreements do not only occur in marriages. Industrial and international relations are fields where ideological interpretations have terrific power to inhibit interaction. The Cold War and industrial disputes have shown this very clearly. It is not just behaviour that is important; the assumed meanings of events act as a screen, and while at one level groups may appear to be interacting, each may be trying systematically to invalidate and to isolate others.

An individual may adopt an ideology which supports his behaviour. Although he might construct it for himself, it is more often accepted as a consequence of some group membership. The basic process therefore involves conformity to or deviance from social influence, and many formal groups exist primarily to promulgate or preserve attitudes towards issues and to smooth out or eliminate disagreements and differences. Consistency, in public behaviour at least, may then be obtained. There are many forms of adherence to groups, many different reasons to be given for membership, and also differences in the kinds of group structure.

Studies of social prejudice have shown that incongruence of belief is a more important determinant of social distance than are ethnic differences. An ideology can be a visible identifying function that influences acceptance or discrimination, and may draw prejudice. So many social differences exist because people believe that they exist, and social assessments are based on these important fictions and judgements (R. Brown, 1965, pp. 115–20, considers the effects of class consciousness). Beliefs and attitudes work to restrict or limit social intercourse, and a person's beliefs become linked to social effects and with his social status. Social affiliation, including church membership, politics and occupation, give a structure that supports an ideology, and socialization into the ideologies of these groups is often involuntary.

Toch (1966) has described several specific ideologies and doctrines that have been expressed in social movements. The necessity for that analysis to be in social terms is emphasized by the fact that members (and especially new members) relate their belonging first to those who are already there and then to the defined ideology.

7 Embodied in Social Movements

Toch (1966) interprets social movements in terms of the members' susceptibility to the influences which the movement's appeals satisfy, and notes that it is the extremes which focus movements. The best examples of social movements are either religious or political. Groups are important agents of social influence and there are many concepts in social psychology that explain cohesion and social control. Among the more obvious are social reinforcement, conformity, balance and its derivatives in dissonance and consistency, social facilitation, norm formation and role prescription, as well as descriptions of motivation and perception, trust or suspicion, communication, leadership, loyalty and group dynamics. A rather naive approach to group functioning is through the explicit purposes that can be served by any group, but the basic processes are in face-to-face interaction and in those effects where institutional and traditional factors are primary.

Cartwright and Zander (1968, p. 306) identified two kinds of groups: those that set out to achieve a specific goal and those concerned simply to maintain themselves. This distinction suggests that groups may be classified as instrumental or expressive, depending on the extent to which an external goal is specified and the ways that success is to be measured. Instrumental groups may have their purposes formulated in ideological terms, with principles or aims that can be accepted and followed and well-defined beliefs. They depend on their capacity to mobilize the support and allegiance of their members who actualize and implement the content and the style of their ideologies. Beyond any explicit purpose, a group may have an authoritarian or a democratic structure (or be in between), and members will differ in their commitment to the group and in the reasons for their attachment.

Social movements may involve one or several, nested groups that share some beliefs that are directed to the solution of a common problem. The members will share varying degrees of satisfaction with, or agreement about, a movement's goals (in which case factions develop) while a movement gives a structure to the behaviour of its members. Many movements have well-identified leaders as well as more remote figures who provide an idealized leadership (like the saints or philosophers), and outsiders and insiders differ in their knowledge and assessment of any movement.

Collective behaviour

There are many bases for collective behaviour. Festinger, Riecken and Schachter (1956) have noted that receiving social support and proselyting other people are two mechanisms that sustain a group. They identified these mechanisms in a study of a real group that was heavily committed to the belief that the world would end with a cataclysm on a certain day. But the bulk of the detailed psychological work on group functioning has been based on artificial or therapeutic groups and not on groups that occur naturally. While experimental groups are transitory, and cannot capture all the features of an enduring group, many groups have a continuing life and persevere despite the changes in their membership.

The natural history of social movements has drawn a continuing interest, and innumerable accounts are available of the aims and the backgrounds of their leaders (e.g. Malcolm X, 1966) or of the wider context written with varying degrees of detachment (Cantril, 1941). There seems recently to have been an increase or change in the general level of awareness about movements, and especially about the more radical ones. This has altered the behaviour of those who are inside these movements, while those outside can more easily generalize their prejudiced responses. Movements deserve highly detailed psychological studies of their derivation, with the forms of support also being carefully traced. Too frequently accounts of a movement's development follow a general theory, and rather simple interpretations are made about the likely social or environmental pressures, often with little firm data. So Parkin (1968, p. 10) asserts that 'Alienation is taken to be the chief characteristic of individuals recruited to mass movements, and the psychological motive force behind their attraction to extremist politics.'

Movements can express or embody some principle, and to account for their genesis and decline becomes the object of analysis. The success of a movement is often attributed to the way it appears to satisfy psychological needs, while the predisposition to join particular groups has been attributed to some 'felt-deprivation' that the group is able to satisfy (Glock and Stark, 1965). This has become a common view of religious groups and especially of some sects, as in Lanternari (1963). In a similar way Maslow distinguished between growth and deficiency needs in his general motivational theory (1954). Inner and outer effects may converge, and a social movement that gave no personal satisfactions would probably fail, although there are many kinds of support that could be given, covering emotional, cognitive or social effects. Other group origins that have been postulated include Smelser's concept of 'generalized beliefs' which is reminiscent of a 'group mind' process, and the models that depend on unconscious factors.

The very early work includes Le Bon and Tarde's analyses of the crowd and 'instincts of the herd'. Early social psychological studies include Cantril's account of a lynching mob. He explored its social setting, demographic character, economic foundation, cultural background and traditions, and its psychological setting and cognitive functions. Cantril notes that 'The conditions which create a lynching mob are deeply interwoven with the whole social context surrounding individual mob members. The norms of the culture . . . largely determine what things people take for granted' (1941, p. 93). Cantril concluded from a similar examination of the Kingdom of Father Divine that it satisfied otherwise unsatisfied needs, provided an escape from material hardships and a new social status. The possible explanations that can be advanced are well exemplified in Cantril's account of the success of the Nazi

Party in the 1930s, which covers psychoanalytic and economic interpretations, the use of mass hypnotic tactics, the innate barbarism of the Germans and the genius of Hitler himself (p. 211 ff.). But Cantril goes on to say that 'The question of *why* the Nazis were successful is not satisfactorily answered for the social psychologist until he has translated the conditions, circumstances and events recorded by others into their psychological consequences for the individuals who supported and who were the Nazi movement' (p. 211). Such data are, unfortunately, almost always inaccessible.

Other studies of relevance to social movements besides Toch's recent text (1966) and the chapter by Milgram and Toch (1969) are Almond's study of communist defectors (1954), and studies of those who have left the Church (Kotre, 1971), are marginal to a parish structure (Fichter, 1953) or who are outside the Church (Vernon, 1968). There are also numerous studies of the recent campus unrest and of student protest, frequently in terms of the *issues* involved. While there may be a shortage of formal data, there is no shortage either of theory or of interest among those in other disciplines about the pressures that build up in groups and in social movements (cf. Gusfield, 1970). Often the theories are tested informally against data derived from the personal accounts of people who have been involved, or from other documentary material about the movement. Any psychological approach requires some direct access to the *people* involved.

Explanations

Many of the explanations can be regarded as fairly obvious. Individuals develop a social identity around their group memberships, and their behaviour is explicitly directed towards defined goals. Committed members accept the group norms, become dependent upon them, and structure their perceptions and cognitions in ways consistent with these processes. But there is still some diversity of response among those who are involved in a social movement, and it is this that gives most interest for psychological study.

Sherif and Sherif (1969) have argued for the separation of

the motivational bases and the ideological bases in studies of social movements. To them the motivational base 'refers to arousal produced by conditions that affect a large number of people simultaneously or within a specifiable period of time' (p. 552). As examples they cite mass deprivation of food, the frustration of living under oppression, subjugation to injustice and denial of rights. These each imply a defined need that the movement attempts to satisfy and which can activate others who have a similar relative deprivation. The ideological base is a convergence of the 'verdicts or slogans' that can express the causes of the ills or the discontent, and is a 'formulation of the premises and rationale of the movement with a platform of changes advocated, and an action strategy to be followed in bringing about the changes' (p. 560). They argue that over time the two bases converge, while the 'formulators of the ideological base are those alienated intellectuals who throw their lot with those who share the motivational base more directly' (p. 560). The distinction between intellectuals and activists is important since some action is specified, unless the movement is simply expressive and lacks any instrumental purpose.

The ideological base seems necessarily to reflect an historical context. Precipitating and long-term factors are required, both to focus the norms of the movement and to provide anchors that direct and control the behaviour. Movements will develop their own differentiated structure, with recognized roles reflecting different levels and forms of motivation among the members, while the leadership mobilizes opinions and guides behaviour.

This analysis presupposes some 'rational' basis for social action, and may be contrasted with the account given by Freud in which affiliation with a social movement was seen as a form of regression to placate powerful and uncontrollable forces. Perhaps it is this theory that made it usual to assume that acceptance of an ideology satisfies profound psychological needs.

Ideological selection

Lane, a political scientist, has advanced a theory of ideological change in which ideologies are assumed to be selected from a range of alternatives in terms of the functions that they serve in meeting the needs of individuals and of groups for orientation, goal attainment and adjustment to others, and in expressing psychic needs and tensions. Ideologies are also selected by their congruence between the experiences both of individuals and groups, their images, ideas and values, unconscious needs and drives, and the conscious programmes for individual behaviour and for group action (1962, p. 442 ff.). Such a formulation is so broad that it probably embraces every possible alternative and contingency. Simpler interpretations may be more useful. Rosenberg points out (in Kelman, 1965, p. 301) that attitudinal certainty and norm formation are produced through a collective experience. Some will find the available reference groups inauthentic and so will join a movement with its own rhetoric and ideology, and with which they can easily relate. Deeply unconscious processes do not need to be introduced as explanations, and anyway they are hard to validate. But individual differences in involvement with social movements should not be underestimated and may be a further reason why unconscious motivations could be introduced as explanations of involvement. Such differences, or more obvious differences in meaning could cause the flux in members' alignments and differentiations that have been often described by the participants or infiltrators of social movements and gangs using an observational method. Observations of crowds or riotous outbursts are an alternative to observation of continuing movements. Social influences are of course involved in them, while interactions are controlled by the cultural forms and the idioms that specify the appropriate patterns of behaviour for these situations. The likelihood that ideological control operates in crowds cannot be simply dismissed (Milgram and Toch, 1969).

Institutional effects

The way that ideas control and direct institutional behaviour can be clearly seen in organizations such as hospitals and the military, both of which have a hierarchical structure. Not only is there an ideological base for these systems, but a bonding or concordance develops between those involved (cf. Blishen,

1969). Some groups or movements may be directed to making a radical change. Groups devoted to natural childbirth provide one example, as does the religio-psychiatric movement (Klausner, 1964). Klausner claims that, as the composition of this movement changed, its ideology changed. He examined change in the norms governing the relationships between ministers and psychiatrists towards their institutions, their clients and to one another, and he distinguishes between 'the ideological stance of the movement as a whole' and the 'ideological positions of the individuals in the movement'. Klausner examined material from 100 individuals who had written at least one book or article in each of the periods 1948–52, 1953–7 and 1958–62. This is a clever adaptation of the conventional panel methods to define the patterns of change within a social movement, and he concludes that the 'religio-psychiatric movement has ceased to be that rebellious challenge to traditional religion and to traditional psychiatry that it had been from its small beginnings at the turn of the century until the 1950s. Both its minister and its psychiatrist members are shoring-up their own institutional allegiances.' Some movements do succeed and may change because they become accepted or because they assumed control of a source of power, whether by legitimate or illegitimate means. Perhaps other movements change simply to be able to continue in existence. But an ideological base seems to be important unless direct coercion and total control can ensure continued adherence to a movement and can repel negative pressures. Persecution may itself perpetuate strong or militant bonds, and studies of the severity of initiation provide a model of these effects (Aronson and Mills, 1959). Specified roles and allegiance can interact to control expressions of an ideological stance, as was shown in the study of workers whose attitudes changed to fit with their positions as foremen or as shop stewards (see page 108). These effects are summarized in the concept of 'participant-regulation'.

Participant-regulation

Cawte (1960) has described how the incidence of identified mental illness in northern Australia is limited by the behaviour and attitudes of the people who run the institutions and organizations that deal with the disorders by the professional (and ideological) allegiances of these people, the attitudes of the patients and specifically their awareness of discomfort and the strength of their demands and expectations for relief, the demands made by relatives, and the attitudes of the community at large. These participants, in their different ways, all collude and so help to regulate the incidence of these illnesses. Cawte rested participant regulation on the 'unconsciously determined attitudes and behaviours of the groups involved'. The concept points up the enormous amount of implicit control that can be exercised through prejudices. Examples of this control can be found in many areas of medicine, including the slow control over puerperal fever in Central Europe during the eighteenth and nineteenth centuries, when the heaviest mortality occurred in unmarried mothers in charity hospitals. It needed an outsider, Semmelweiss, who was a Hungarian working in Vienna, to force change in the procedures and so to check the sepsis that was being transmitted, the cause of which had actually been recognized. Interpretations about, and the treatments for, schizophrenia give another example of participant regulation and of the application of ideologies to explain, interpret and provide for these patients. The fashion for prefrontal leucotomy that peaked around 1950 is a further example, of which Cawte writes, 'The onslaught (to the frontal lobes) will suggest to many people that feelings of aggression and mastery, stirred up in war, overflowed on mental patients.' The arguments advanced against its use covered ethical, religious and psychodynamic considerations, and show the breadth of concern that is needed to effect some changes.

In each of these examples there are two levels of interpretation: the explicit and rational, and the psychodynamic and covert. Perhaps these correspond to the ideological and the motivational bases identified by Sherif and Sherif as the roots for other social movements. Maybe it is the prevalent availability of the term 'ideology', and its now common use as an explanation by itself, that has facilitated a recognition of the current forms of social protest. This recognition has undoubtedly been facilitated by the communication styles of the mass media.

Social change

Social contexts, issues and accepted doctrines, as well as the active pressure groups, are all changing, and accepted truths lie behind an ideology and behind the movements that gain their unity and direction through an ideology. Group behaviour implies positive and negative attitudes among those involved, experiences of frustration or gratification, of success and failure, and relationships of superiority and inferiority. These feelings will not necessarily influence all members of a group but, when they do impinge uncomfortably, people begin to defect or to change their status in other ways. Although there has been a recurrent tendency to interpret group behaviour in terms of its effects on individuals, the properties of groups themselves need to be emphasized. So Klineberg (1954) noted that acts of violence among lynching groups do not necessarily occur more frequently in societies where individual frustrations are greater, but Swanson (1960) found that monotheistic religious systems are to be found in cultures where power is distributed among social groups.

We can take it that questions about intra- and inter-group behaviour, both crucial in social movements, are not so much concerned with various abnormalities as with participation and conformity within groups. Interpretations predominantly in terms of personality require too great an extrapolation of intra-psychic factors. The capacity of movements to mobilize individuals and to structure their behaviour may provide a better basis for interpretation than does an interpretation of the attractiveness of ideologies to individuals. In the absence of conclusive data, we must emphasize that social movements have an important role in expressing, preserving and developing ideologies.

A further explanation comes from the reference functions and the ways a consensus develops and produces both the beliefs and the responses that are to be made. Research on social judgement has shown unequivocally the extent to which anchors and norms are fixed by group processes, whether in judgements of physical properties, or about values. Groups also develop norms and constraints that prescribe the rules for the control of behaviour. Schachter (1965), for example, showed that responses to physiological arousal are interpreted from the cues and the information that is available in the behaviour of others in the environment. So the physiological state resulting from an injection of epinephrine may be labelled 'joy' or 'fury', depending on the cognitive and the social definition of the situation in which it is administered. To extrapolate, we can suggest that the feelings derived from other specific stimuli or situations themselves will be influenced by environmental factors, and by the norms that control responsiveness. Much also depends on the explanations that are available.

Accounts of social movements often emphasize the extent to which social interaction is influenced by an ideology and by a group's own functioning, and within which differentiation develops. In his study of developing acquaintance, Newcomb (1961) described the importance of value similarities in developing interpersonal attraction. He also showed the interdependence of liking and value similarities in attraction and agreement, although these elements are separate only for the convenience of their analysis. Newcomb agrees with Heider that groups are in balance if interpersonal attraction is high *and* there is agreement about 'important matters'. Just as cognitions need to be balanced, so the members of a group must be in some equilibrium. Agreement can be based on myths and generalized responses, and may obscure characteristics of the people behind their facades. Ideas about masculinity and femininity, of self-expression and self-control, of independence and respect for authority, or of rich and poor rely on an exaggerated opposition, and the stereotyped explanations developed about these characteristics feed their exaggeration.

Environmental control

A person's view of the environment mediates his social behaviour as he aims for some control over it. 'Total environments' in Goffman's sense, like prisons, embody an ideology from which there is little possibility of dissent, with acquiescence necessary. Conformity then should not be misconstrued as allegiance, since there are distinctions between public and private compliance (McGuire, 1969, p. 239). Cantril (1941) similarly separated the role of the environmental context from motivational factors and from the 'particular pattern of pre-dispositions influencing the individual at the moment' (p. xii). Each of these separate factors limits the opportunities for an ideology to structure behaviour.

A social movement is therefore characterized by a patterning of social norms about what is or should be, and is limited by 'desires, worries, frustrations and prejudices' (Cantril, 1941, p. 5). Different sets of conditions can be examined, one of which is the stable system into which a person is socialized and which brings his outlook into line with that of some group.

In a study of two contrasted student religious groups, it was found that the more liberal group's members were homo-geneous with respect to political beliefs but heterogeneous with respect to their religious beliefs, while the more conservative group's members were heterogeneous in their political beliefs and homogeneous religiously (Brown, 1962a). In that study the leaders were not specially identified, nor were any casual outsiders included.

Marx and Useem (1971) made a comparative assessment of three social movements following the 'themes' of ideological disagreements between the insiders and the outsiders, the divergent background and experience of the activists who structure the movements, the cultural conflicts so that 'sus-picion, distrust and scapegoating on the part of the minority group and stereotyping, patronization and paternalism on the part of the dominant group have often resulted', and finally the development of these conflicts over time. The movements they studied related to civil rights and anti-slavery in the US and the abolition of untouchability in India, as examples of inter-group clashes in which ideological factors facilitated a demarcation and mobilization of opinion. Contemporary social and political events have made such effects almost commonplace, while the activists themselves become more rigid and committed, perhaps as a result of their public stand. The leaders regard differences between insiders and outsiders as critical, while the insiders differ in their levels of understanding and in their identities. One way to explore some of these factors might be to take a movement and contrast the members who foster its ideology but have little relevant experience against those who have the relevant and direct experience. These contrasts are to be found among the members of movements for prison reform, homosexual law reform, marriage and/or abortion law reform. Such a study might show the ways that a developed ideology depends on some interpretations of experience or perhaps rests primarily on questions of principle. Lenin believed that the intellectual in a working-class movement was an outsider with a critical role in the class struggle since he could offer a generalized critique of the social order; in this role he could be more radical than the workers and might perhaps be analogous to the psychotherapist who stands apart yet can offer interpretations. Leaders and followers are likely to put different constructions on their social involvement, although the leaders usually have control. While a group member may adhere strongly to the group's ideology or to the group itself, decisions can be made with which he might disagree but to which he must conform for various reasons. He may then try to exercise an undue influence and assume control. When he is unsuccessful, he will change his involvement and so may defect.

Leadership

Apart from their skills and knowledge, leaders have been found to differ from their followers in several ways, but not much in their personality characteristics. This aspect was pursued in the early work on leadership and produced rather inconsistent results because of the differences between groups, and the emphasis has moved now to the place of group functions and skills. Cultures may differ in their tolerance of different styles of leadership and in the accepted forms of group control, as the contrasts between the communist and the capitalist countries with their obvious differences between authoritarian and democratic forms have shown (Korten, 1962). Rose (1962) in a study of the leaders of state-wide organizations in Minnesota in 1959 found them to have a higher education, and to be more frequently in professional or managerial occupations and of higher social status than was the general population. (This 'participation' *may* itself be a kind of personality trait.) The leaders were found to be more involved socially and to have a greater realism, lesser alienation and more definite ideas about their personal aspirations than the general population.

Enduring groups have too often been investigated with a 'one-shot' approach to define the attitudes or the personality characteristics of their members, rather than to specify the principles they rest on and the forms of their coherence. The group dynamics literature that derived from the study of combat groups and gangs and from work with experimentally constructed groups (Cartwright and Zander, 1968) has provided many interpretations and hypotheses that could be tested in enduring groups or movements. A psychologist's primary interest is, however, to evaluate social movements against the relationships of the individual members in them, whether in terms of the satisfactions that are offered, their psychological consequences, or the forms of affiliation. In every movement there are probably differences between leaders and followers, between strong and weak, and between the privileged and the others. These differences depend on power and influence, and on status and respect, and are supported by ideologies about justice, freedom, or control, as explanatory systems that help to force compliance, and from which the individual escapes only with difficulty.

Membership

Within religious contexts, there have been many suggestions about the ways in which individuals affiliate with institutions and with belief systems. These have been summarized by Brown (1964) and include distinctions between intrinsic and extrinsic (Allport, 1966), committed and consensual (Allen and Spilka, 1967) and institutional and individual orientations.

In a content analysis of the replies to a set of open-ended questions about the reasons for holding religious beliefs,

Brown found that the answers fell into several categories that appeared to lie on two dimensions. 'The first corresponds to Allport's intrinsic–extrinsic dimension and specifies the role or function of belief, while the second covers institutionalization and individualism and concerns the manner of accepting beliefs or the role of authority in the acceptance or rejection of any belief–disbelief system' (Brown, 1964).

Whatever the process and the reasons for involvement, the forms of identification within a movement and the relationships between members all contribute to its character and even to its likely success. An ideology that can objectify issues for a movement might well produce a different kind of involvement from one that is protective and merely involves self-interest. But the motivations to be found among the members of a social movement have still not been well studied.

8 Explained through Personality

A continuing question in personality theory has concerned the effects of personality variables and processes on the acceptance of, or susceptibility to, attitudes and ideologies, and not only to those that are in some degree deviant. So in a recent review of a book on the Panthers, Marx (1972) writes,

To explain why the original Black Panthers in Oakland became involved in political violence, while other similar groups in that city did not, one must look not so much at the personalities of the Panthers as to how the government came to define them as a threat, and their subsequent labelling and treatment as a dangerous revolutionary group.

William James believed that philosophies are a function of the philosophers' temperaments, and in his discussion of *Pragmatism* (1907) he especially contrasted those who were system builders against those with a more empirical interest. There is now considerable sophistication in the terms that are available. Anyone who might believe that social power is important is thought to be compensating, and one who encourages censorship may be rationalizing a prurient interest. But one needs a theory to explain how any behaviour will be interpreted. There are good games to be played in applying the psychoanalytic mechanisms of defence to make interpretations, but they are still very difficult to test objectively. Interpretations like these are of course to be found most clearly in the writings of Freud. He regarded religion for example as an externalization or projection of unconscious conflicts; as the illusion of a father who provides happiness in heaven in return for a renunciation of instinctual drives now. Evidence for a predicted similarity between the content of beliefs about God and the content of parental images does not, however, support Freud's predictions. The trend is in fact towards a similarity between the images of mother and of God (Gorsuch, 1968). In contrast to Freud's theory, Swanson (1960), as we have noted, has summarized material from the Human Relations Area Files which suggests that differences between a society's beliefs about its gods are closely tied to social structure, and that ideas about the supernatural spring from experiences of persisting sovereign groups in a society. There are many different levels of explanation.

Individuals have unique experiences that become tied with their beliefs and these have led to hypotheses about the general or specific processes that may have caused them. So Lasswell attempted 'to show that attitudes favourable to revolt against established institutional practices were associated with aggression against the father', while Krout and Stagner found 'in their radical subjects more frequent feelings of rejection by their parents and in general more unhappiness in childhood than in a control group' (cited by Eysenck, 1954, p. 191). The study of authoritarianism and of 'potentially fascistic individuals' has become a model for accounts of the interaction between social and personality dynamics, but those findings raise questions about the relationships between personality and social and family influences, and about the ways that they can be mediated by child-rearing techniques. Eysenck in his turn argued that extraverted parents have tough attitudes which cause them to engage in authoritarian child-rearing, and through which their children inherit both an extraverted personality and tough social attitudes (1954, p. 196).

Personality theories

There are many personality theories. All share the fact that they assign a crucial role to motivational processes while differing in the dimensions and the components that they stress. Some theories are structured and rest on traits, while others are more functional. To exemplify the range, consider Rosenblatt's (1964) inventory of propositions that relate to ethnocentrism and nationalism; he distinguishes group-based explanations (including manipulation by a leader) from explanations that stress psychic needs. He writes that 'ethnocentrism and nationalism may provide rewards stemming from increased satisfaction of needs for affiliation with something relatively unique, strong or enduring, needs for affiliation with other individuals similar to one, needs for affiliation with some cause, needs for cognitive efficiency or simplicity, needs to justify selfish desires, needs to retaliate aggressively or to displace aggression, needs to reduce boredom, needs to think well of one's self and needs for the familiar.' He sets out to predict 'which members of the group are most ethnocentric or nationalistic' and concludes that they are the insecure and the marginal members, or those who stand to profit. There are many fairly obvious difficulties in the way of establishing the validity of these interpretations, including the problems of sampling and of measurement.

A primary task for personality study has been to account for individual differences, but there is now considerable evidence that situational factors like roles and other prescribed behaviours take up much more of the variance in individuals' responses to situations than do their individual differences (Endler, Hunt and Rosenstein, 1962). The way this effect works in generating or shaping ideas has yet to be settled, but the likely results might show that learning and other associative effects produce most consistency in these responses. Nevertheless, personality-based explanations have persevered and typically assume that beliefs are derived from a prior state and are not simply learnt. Another alternative theory assumes that people have the ability to think logically and can assess situations, but that these processes get out of phase when emotional or affective elements are superimposed on to the content. It is therefore argued that the distorted responses show some personality-based involvement. Ordinary introspection, as well as casual observation suggests that strong feelings can develop around cognitions, and especially around those that are related to social issues. Although simple introspective material cannot be used to make systematic tests, it does point to the kinds of commitment and some of the specific meanings that develop around beliefs and attachments to ideas.

Ideologies are involved in the personality theories themselves. A value for intense present experiences can explain motivated behaviour (as in the Dionysian value identified by Kluckhohn and Strodtbeck, 1961) perhaps as much as does Skinner's theory of the environmental control over behaviour. Maybe some differences between theories rest simply on the metaphors that are used to describe behaviour. So Weiss (1963) gave an account of recruitment to, and defection from, social movements in Hullian terms using the processes of simple stimulus generalization, extinction, displacement (owing to inhibition by approach–avoidance conflict) and counter-conditioning.

Variables

Marlowe and Gergan (1969, p. 603) list as the 'personality and individual-difference dimensions' cognitive complexity, internal $v.$ external feelings of control, manifest anxiety, role constructs, ego strength, Machiavellianism, open- $v.$ closed-mindedness, repression $v.$ sensitization, and self-disclosure. These, and other variables like conformity, persuasibility, dominance and achievement, can be related to ideological styles, and even to specific ideologies, although the detailed exploration of many of these relationships is still to be carried out. To ask for psychological roots is common enough, but it can lead to rather barren tracks and the simple answers are in terms of sovereign drives, with implicit assumptions about their priorities. Few sets of drives cover all cases, unless it is a 'need to explain or to understand', or in terms like adjustment, social interaction, and competence. In general, an explanation in terms of needs refers to the continuing influence of internal states, and avoids the problem of how these definite patterns can link attitudes with personality. The relationships may be direct, or either one can predispose the other. It may even be that the personality processes like extraversion which reflect styles of interpersonal behaviour, are more important influences on ideologies than are the intra-psychic processes. Other theories have invoked historical effects and the intellectual influences to which people have been exposed, or specify the implicit attractiveness that certain beliefs have to those with defined personality characteristics or predispositions.

In considering the relationships between beliefs and personality, the possibility should be considered that beliefs themselves can form a personality, and can even limit a man's potential. Restricted attitudes to, for example, sexual morality may well constrict social interaction. Marx makes a similar point when he says, 'What makes them representatives of the petty bourgeoisie is the fact that in their minds they do not exceed the limits which the latter do not exceed in their life activities' (quoted by Merton, 1968, p. 517). There are variants of this view in other material. Merton cites an early paper by Fromm who 'attempted to show that Freud's "conscious liberalism" tacitly involved a rejection of impulses tabooed by bourgeois society and that Freud was himself, in his patricentric character, a typical representative of a society which demands obedience and subjection' (Merton, 1968, p. 540).

Argument about the relative importance of social and personality explanations may be similar to ideological debates about the relative contribution of environment and heredity, and different ideologies have dominated the analysis of personality. Burnham (1968) has described the historical background to contemporary studies of personality and identifies the positions that have been adopted to explain or represent 'the nature of man and his individuality' (1968, p. 1). These *ideas* about personality, character and temperament, and their doctrinaire nature can now be easily recognized in the seventeenth-century disputes about a mechanistic physiology and environmentalism on the one hand, and the forms of rationalism on the other. Later the Revolutionary French ideologues believed that 'life cannot be reduced to physical and chemical processes but includes a life force' (1968, p. 29), yet they also saw mind as a physical or bodily function. We are not now involved with these theories, nor with the later nineteenth-century views about physiognomy, phrenology or the forms of instinct. Perspective on them might suggest that current attempts at an empirical approach to personality may come to be seen as similarly ideological. Eysenck's criticism of the

Freudian theory, called 'What is wrong with psychoanalysis?' (1953), uses arguments about the nature of science and the forms of evidence to support his attack. The writings of R. D. Laing (already a cult figure) have been reviewed by Tyson (1971) who found a shift or progression from the view in *The Divided Self* that one part of the self repudiates another, to locating 'the enemy' in pathological communication within the family, and finally to the 'strait jacket of conformity' that is imposed on children at their birth. Arguments about the basis of intelligence have also taken on an ideological or political character and, in an attempt at resolution, more than one kind of intelligence has been posited (Vernon, 1969) to cover the innate level, the realized or achieved level and the measured level. Jensen's argument about the biological or racial basis of intellectual differences has elicited irrationally strong feelings. Brazziel (1969), in 'A letter from the South' asks what social policies become a consequence of this view, and talks of a 'white intellectual supremacy'. There is also the letter signed by fifty eminent psychologists on 'Behaviour and heredity' in the *American Psychologist*, 1972, vol. 27, pp. 660–61. Among other points, they 'deplore the evasion of hereditary reasoning in current textbooks.' We have already noted ideological factors in some practices of medicine and psychiatry and in beliefs about the causes of nervous or mental diseases or in views about alcoholism.

Political personalities

Established traditions have set out to identify the general characteristics of those with defined political attitudes. Thus Moore in 1929 reported that radicals excelled in the ability to break established habits which he measured by mirror-drawing, and were superior to conservatives in producing unusual word associations on the Kent–Rosanoff list. In a similar way, Lindner (1953) said that communists have neurotic problems, often guilt related, while fascists are psychopaths and have underdeveloped consciences. These analyses seemed to disregard the social context within which political affiliations develop. Even with a recognition of context, there is still the implication that the effects are unreal and irrational, as when Lasswell (1960, especially pp. 65–77) uses an interpretation of 'displaced affect rationalized in the public interest'. In contrast to this assumed irrationalism, Asch (1952) stressed the information that is positively available in a group's consensus as another way that ideologies can link individuals with society.

The Authoritarian Personality was concerned with the congruence between a personality type and a political ideal, and it gave a stimulus to studies of the relationships between personality and social attitudes. Although the original study was based on a broadly psychoanalytic theory, it applied other concepts about personality, like repression–sensitization, externalization–internalization, conventionalism–genuineness, power–orientation–love–orientation and rigidity–flexibility. The guiding hypothesis was 'that the political, economic and social conviction of an individual often forms a broad and coherent pattern . . . and that this pattern is an expression of deep-lying trends in his personality' (Adorno *et al.*, 1950, p. 1). The study was directed at the 'potentially fascistic individual' as a recognized syndrome of personality and ideology, chosen for study because of its social relevance at a time of threat from fascism and anti-semitism. Among their conclusions, Adorno *et al.*, state that

a basically hierarchical, authoritarian, exploitive parent–child relationship is apt to carry over into a power-oriented, exploitively dependent attitude towards one's sex partner and one's God and may well culminate in a political philosophy and social outlook which has no room for anything but a desperate clinging to what appears to be strong and a disdainful rejection of whatever is relegated to the bottom. The inherent dramatization likewise extends from the parent–child dichotomy to the dichotomous conception of sex roles and moral values. . . . Conventionality, rigidity, repressive denial and the ensuing breakthrough of one's weakness, fear and dependency are but other aspects of the same personality pattern, and they can be observed in personal life as well as in attitudes towards religion and social issues (1950, p. 971).

They found the prejudiced to be more homogeneous than he unprejudiced, and the task of eliminating prejudice was said to be like that of 'eliminating neurosis, delinquency or nationalism from the world'. They dealt with 'dynamic potentials' rather than overt behaviour (p. 972), and refer to prejudice or ethnocentricity as both a 'disease' and 'a structure within the person' (p. 974). Although the authors argue against any one-to-one correspondence between personality and ideology in particular cases, it was their efforts to relate ideology to personality that made the California study of Authoritarianism 'strikingly original' (R. Brown, 1965, p. 481). Personality was treated 'as an organization of needs varying in quality, intensity and object' (1965, p. 481), and one characteristic of their prejudiced subjects was to express ego-alien feelings, or to project feelings of sex and aggression (as in the man who said 'I have let my carnal self get away from me', 1965, p. 500). Another defence mechanism that operated was displacement, so that external events are blamed when things go wrong. They concluded that a severe family training frustrated and so created aggression among the prejudiced people. Authoritarianism has also been identified as a cognitive style, with effects on perceptual rigidity (Frenkel-Brunswick, 1954).

Many controversies stemmed from the theory of the authoritarian personality. One was the extent to which personality and acceptance of an ideology could be treated as *identical*, so that 'authoritarianism' can refer to both a set of beliefs about the nature of society and to a personality orientation. This is not an unusual theory. Whiting and Child (1953, p. 65) consider that 'customs' and the belief that incantations cause illness are 'indices of the adult personality traits characteristic of a society'. In this form, the relationships between ideology and personality become so close that any characterization of an ideology is a statement about the modal personality within a culture. This can be illustrated by the interpretation that a fear of sorcerers in a given culture means 'that the typical member of the society fears the direct expression of aggression' (Inkeles and Levinson, 1969, p. 434). It is almost too easy to reduce any belief proposition to an expression of some personality trait.

Criticisms of authoritarianism

Roger Brown's chapter 10 (1965) gives a thorough account of work on the authoritarian personality. He notes that the Berkeley researchers were concerned with ideology which they thought of as an organization of opinions, attitudes and values, in political, economic and religious spheres (p. 481) and with personality 'which they thought of in the Freudian tradition, as an organization of needs varying in quality, intensity and object' (p. 481). Their argument was supported by evidence of covariation across several fixed alternative and projective measures. The vital criticisms that Brown notes relate to the too wide generalization of their conclusions, the problem of acquiescence response set in their measures and the problem of the content analyses of the interview and the TAT material, as well as a lack of control of other intervening factors that might be operating. These included intelligence, education and socio-economic status.

The earlier detailed criticisms of this work influenced and refined the subsequent development of social psychology. Brown's general conclusion is that 'dynamic interrelations as well as the ties with status and education – cooperate to hold this mosaic together' (p. 526). 'This mosaic' is one of attitudes and personality. The question whether there is an authoritarian-ism of the left later raised the question of dogmatism, as a more general trait, and Brown's general conclusion is that the basic similarities that Adorno *et al.*, investigated were ideo-logical. Others have noted the 'ideological blindness' of their analysis.

Himmelweit and Swift have reported a study in which 400 subjects in England responded to measures of authoritarianism when they were aged 13–14, and again when they were aged 24–25. Among the adolescents they found differences according to ability level, with the more able showing the greater stability of response across time. It is argued from this study that the general concept of authoritarianism breaks down to several discrete factors, with especial differentiations between an authoritarian view of society, an authoritarian view of parental rule, a 'pro containment and status quo' and a 'jaundiced view of life' focused among adults on work relations. The authoritarian view of society and the *pro status quo* factors were the only ones that were stable across time.

Social character

Some social issues may be more critical than others for the involvement they show with forms of personality functioning. Inkeles and Levinson (1969) argue that for this reason relations to authority and conceptions of the self are 'standard analytic issues'. Other core concepts might derive from analyses of the effects of organizational patterns, from political, economic and status structures, from ecological factors, sociocultural factors, or from social change (1969, p. 470). Prevalent social opinions may either foster or inhibit the development of some personality patterns. So a trait of benevolence might be fostered by certain kinds of religious (or moral) training (1969, p. 479), and aggressiveness could be developed by a school's procedures and discipline. Religious beliefs have been asserted to be particularly vulnerable to the effects of personality involvement.

Studies of the factorial composition of religious beliefs in relation to personality tend to show a single religious–belief factor that has no relationship with personality measures, and yet it is strongly related to affiliation with a church. The other factors that are extracted depend on both the particular measures and the samples used. In one study (Brown, 1962b) a second factor covered personality effects in anxiety and neuroticism and related to certainty about political opinions and about general factual questions, but not to the strength of religious belief. The single religious–belief factor has however been broken down to many *theoretically* separate components that cover different kinds of content.

Allport noted that 17,953 English terms designate distinctive and personal forms of behaviour, and that 4504 of them designate 'real traits of personality' (1937, pp. 303 ff.). While it might be possible to specify the conditions that can facilitate the acquisition of these traits, cross-cultural studies of their development and influence point to some limits on their expression. In a similar way, occupational or other social roles control, or interact with, expressed personality characteristics. The causal sequence of these effects may be hard to specify, and those people with defined traits could be being selected into certain roles, while some subtle predispositions might be shaped by the demands of other roles, in much the same way as expressed attitudes can conform to role demands.

Inkeles and Levinson (1969, p. 490) observe that 'many writers seem to assume that national character operates as a simple and direct cause of certain institutions.' In support they cite Gorer's generalizations about the 'older brother' responsibility of the American Senate in comparison with the 'younger brother' House of Representatives, as well as La Barre's work on the Chinese, in which a satisfactory oral relationship established during early personality development was said to be connected 'with the magnificent "sanity" and hard-headedness of the Chinese' with 'the genius of Chinese political philosophy', and with the alleged absence of aggressive warfare in the history of China' (1969, p. 490). These examples are typical of an emphasis on the cumulative social effects of personality, acquired through the consistencies of child rearing. The norms governing child rearing certainly ensure continuity in a culture, and may also implicate the ideologies that circulate within that culture. Inkeles and Levinson note that when no causal relationship is defined, 'an assumption of isomorphism between personality modes and institutional patterns is questionable and begs the real issue.' They go on to say that 'We must study the psychological meaning of partici-pation for the actual participants in a sociocultural process if we are to establish with any confidence the connection between personality modes and the given institutional pattern' (1969, p. 491). These meanings require far more study than they have yet been given.

Weber's analysis linked observations about character and ideology with social processes, by specifically connecting Protestantism with the rise of capitalism. McClelland has extended this scheme to personality functioning and he suggested a mediating social-psychological mechanism that could lie between Weber's terms. From the protestant ideology he identified the parental norms that stress achievement, self-reliance and self-denial, and the related training in early independence and mastery. These all contribute to a development of the high achievement motivation in children that can become a dominant trait or dynamic within personality. The ideology influences the ways in which children are trained, and this leads to the development of related behaviours in adults that are therefore built into early personality functioning. McClelland's theory has been tested against psychological, sociological and economic data. Use of the TAT to measure need achievement has already been described (page 37) and so has the analysis of the themes in children's story books to give a guide to expected levels of achievement motivation in countries known to differ in their economic growth (page 93). This theory has therefore linked into a coherent syndrome several apparently unrelated variables, including religious affiliation, ideology, child training, gross national product, social roles and personality processes in achievement motivation.

The personality analyses that we have mentioned so far emphasize ideological links either through personality dynamics and defence mechanisms *or* through personality traits that relate directly to social behaviour.

Irrational behaviour

Another common set of personality descriptions is derived from psychiatric contexts and from the abnormalities of behaviour. Some findings from essentially clinical studies of individuals are to be considered later, and Katz's functional theory of social attitudes defines the purposes that attitudes may serve (see page 20). He advanced his theory as a compromise between the extreme views that man is entirely irrational with unconscious grounds for his behaviour, and the view that puts man's behaviour entirely under cognitive control; Katz said that 'The second approach is that of the ideologist who invokes a rational model of man' (1960, p. 457). In considering a commitment to nationalism, Katz has further identified symbolic, normative, functional and ideological factors (1965).

Asch advocates a cognitive approach, and characterized the irrational view as follows:

Inspired by psychiatric ideas, psychologists have asserted that adult social attitudes are essentially an indirect expression of personal emotional problems of earlier origin. They have adopted the general proposition that the earliest interpersonal relations of childhood establish enduring character-dispositions that control the adults' orientation to social issues. This proposition takes the emotional structure of the individual as the independent variable and derives social attitudes from it (1952, p. 607).

It is clear that there are likely to be great individual differences in the reasons advanced for adopting either attitudes or ideologically defined positions. But any review of these studies over the last twenty years shows a change from the psycho-dynamic emphasis of the authoritarian personality to a recognition of the importance of cognitive processes, especially in consistency theory (Abelson *et al.*, 1968; Feldman, 1966). Even assuming that there is a personality base for attitudes and ideology, its expression may be modified by other processes like intelligence or knowledge. The 'weights of the mediators will tend to vary from situation to situation in predictable ways', says McGuire (1968) and so personality processes become confounded, and several effects correlate with any single variable that can be isolated.

The recognized differences between psychologists who themselves favour either conventional measurement, experimentation or a clinical approach could itself provide data for a study of the relationships between personality and ideology.

Personality effects have been seen in psychodynamic terms, in terms of consistent structures of behaviour, or as a residual once social and situational factors have been excluded. Although people must express aspects of themselves, if not in the specific content of their beliefs at least in the general positions they adopt and become committed to, there is still great ambiguity. A person who bigotedly supports a particular position may be doing so because of social pressures and influences, or because of an inner dynamic process which forces this response. Issues are available, and it is the (internal) responses that fix their salience. So individuals who differ in their sensitivity to and awareness of ideologies may be responding superficially, or may be exhibiting a more fundamental, even unwitting attachment. Public issues allow idiosyncratic processes and motivations to operate under either internal or external control.

Locus of control

Rotter's analysis of the internal or external control of reinforcement may help to resolve some dilemmas about the forms of this support and influence. He says, 'People in American culture have developed generalized expectancies in learning situations in regard to whether or not reinforcement, reward or success in these situations is dependent upon their own behaviour or is controlled by external forces, particularly luck, chance, or experimenter control, which are fairly consistent from individual to individual' (1966). Rotter devised a scale with twenty-nine forced-choice items and six filler items to measure these orientations. As evidence for its construct validity he shows that a person with 'a strong belief that he can control his own destiny' has attributes that include being able to abstract from the environment information that will be useful for his future behaviour, and being resistive to subtle attempts to influence him.

Rotter's concepts have been applied to ideologies of race among negroes. Gurin *et al.*, (1969) studied the motivational dynamics of negro youth, and identified individual and system blame, on the basis of whether a black person gives individual qualities or social factors as the key determinant of his own fate. Gurin was primarily concerned to answer the question whether an ideology of social control among blacks in the United States involves personality processes, and she noted that Rotter's inventory has two types of item: some relate to the person's own life ('Trusting to fate has never turned out as well for me as making a decision to take a definite course of action') and some to people in general ('Capable people who fail to become leaders have not taken advantage of their opportunities'). She also noted that external control blames chance or a faulty system, and that different ideologies are involved in the contrast between individual and system blame. This is reminiscent of the Rosenzweig frustration–aggression hypothesis, which identified the techniques for dealing with aggression as intrapunitive, extrapunitive and impunitive. Institutions differ in the extent to which they actually facilitate these forms of response, so Catholics have been seen as extrapunitive and Protestants as intrapunitive (Brown, 1965). Rosenzweig's intrapunitive person might also be found to occupy a lowly position in a social system and so be self-depreciating in his evaluation of himself.

Gurin *et al.* administered Rotter's scale to a large sample of negroes in twelve colleges, together with three items from the Institute for Social Research's Personal Efficiency Scale, and a set of other questions in the same forced-choice format to tap beliefs about the operation of personal and external forces in the US racial situation. The data were factor analysed. The first factor was an 'external-control ideology' factor, with only one item in it that explicitly used the first person. The second factor covered personal control, and factor three was labelled 'system modifiability' with the items that define it referring to the control or influence of racial discrimination, war and world affairs. Factor four contained most of the race-related items and, when re-factored it produced a factor labelled 'individual-system blame'. The separation of self from others found among the negroes was not found in the factor analytic results from white populations, since beliefs about internal control cannot often be applied in the blacks' own life situations. The negroes and the whites converged in endorsing general cultural beliefs in terms of the 'Protestant Ethic ideology'.

An external orientation allows 'more effective behaviours' if it can be translated into action. So the work of Paige had shown that 'rioting is clearly associated with rejecting a set of beliefs about the "culture of subordination" in which self-blame rather than system blame is central' (in Gurin, 1969). Rotter's measure of internal and external control shows a personality-based distinction, *if* personality relates to or is expressed through some general expectancies about behaviour. It might also be expected to relate to personality processes like alienation, competence and ego-strength.

There are other translations of social variables into personality terms. Neal and Seeman (1964) developed a scale of powerlessness from Rotter's theory, to assess belief in control over societal and economic problems compared with control over personal problems. This measure, and others that relate to alienation, are discussed by Robinson and Shaver (1969, chapter 4), including Srole's measure that has already been considered (page 41). McClosky and Schaar (1965) developed a measure of anomie, and argued that cognitive and emotional factors and beliefs and opinions impede an individual's learning of acceptable social norms. They reported that 'individual's predisposed to maladjustive emotional states (such as inflexibility, strong anxiety and aggression, and low ego strength) are high on anomie.' Other scales reviewed by Robinson and Shaver recognize the distinction between incapability and discontent, between powerlessness and an awareness of some menacing power. Keniston (1960) has reported in detail on the personalities and values of a group of uncommitted or alienated students.

An integrated view must realize that expressions of attitude and belief involve consistent forms of behaviour and, granted that the measures are usually in a verbal form, there is an interchange between concepts that imply a social orientation and those that imply a personality disposition. Trouble arises when either logical or psychological priority is assigned to one or another process, so that personality processes are claimed to *cause* attitudes. Conceptual refinement is needed to identify the levels at which personality processes are invoked, but there is no shortage either of classifications or of terms that can be applied.

Implicit theories

One conclusion forced by this material is that attitudes can either express personality-based needs, or can express a social value and aspects of social reality. Christie (1956a) noted that 'Any attempt to relate personality variables to political ideology without taking the social context into account is apt to be highly misleading as well as an over-simplification of some highly complex interrelationships' (1956a, p. 428). But there are persistent questions about the kinds of people who believe whatever is to be believed. This suggests a strong and implicit theory about origins, and reminds one of Freud's question about the kind of person who could believe that the middle of the Earth is made of jam. A basic task for any individual is to integrate and develop a rational, realistic understanding of the social and political world. Thus Smith, Bruner and White (1956, p. 275) write of striking a 'compromise between reality demands, social demands and inner psychological demands'. This is similar to Katz's classification of reality-testing motives, value-expressive, social–acceptance and ego-defensive motives for holding social attitudes.

Almond (1954) reported marked differences between middle-class and working–class members in their patterns of motivation into the Communist Party. At interview, the former were characterized by a high incidence of neuroticism and the latter were not. Almond also reported that personality differences were related to the role that the person played in the Party. We are here back with the fact that although personality differences have an important place, they are not independent of the critical social factors that are operating in any situation. Thus social and historical factors may cause people to join a communist party or other ideologically defined group, and personality processes will explain very little. If they were to account for more of the variance, impossible questions would arise about the ways in which people are selected into organizations and groups. To talk of a communist personality or a religious personality, neglects too many of the complex social processes that are involved in developing any ideological position.

Protesters

Despite these strictures, conservatism in both social and personality terms has been well documented, especially in the demonstration of affinities between conservatism and disvalued personality and social characteristics. Bay (1970) argues that the frequency of neurotic motivations is greater for those on the right or conservative side of the political spectrum because these people are restricted and less influenced by the demands of social reality. But there is an ideological, evaluative flavour to his argument. Writing of students, he says that 'the more intensely or neurotically one is preoccupied with career worries, the less one would be disposed to mingle with the student rebels.' These rebels are, he assumes, emancipated and therefore can work to alter and improve the society. Such an assessment might reflect some of the investigator's values. Bay goes on to note that

As rebels, they are more likely to have made a choice and to have marshalled the intellectual and emotional resources, at some point, to stick to it, also in situations of severe stress. Obviously some will for spurious or chance reasons pursue neurotic social acceptance needs with free-speech-movement-type groups as their reference systems; but this happens in almost every group, and is likely to occur with less frequency in a rebellious political–action group than in less demanding and socially more homogeneous groups like, for example, fraternities or sororities . . . (1970, p. 83).

One has heard those who are unsympathetic to the revolting students argue that these students are psychopathic, inadequately socialized, out only to destroy, with nothing positive to replace what they have destroyed. Disputes about them must be informed with data and it is increasingly being found that student activists are intelligent, academically competent, from affluent family backgrounds of liberal political views and idealistic values which coincide with the students' own flexible and self-actualizing values. This is in contrast to the earlier picture of the activists as sick and trying to escape their own problems (Middlebrook, 1972). Patterns of attitudes and beliefs probably alter with age, and studies of age-related change should have an important place in defining the fit between personality and belief, just as what it means to be a radical may change over time.

Kotre (1971) made a comparative study of students raised as Catholics who felt that they had left the Church, and others also raised as Catholics who still considered themselves to be inside the Church. One important conclusion was that the 'Ins' and 'Outs' acknowledged the same evidence. Both 'pointed out unacceptable or irrelevant doctrines', both mentioned racism among Catholics; both regarded with disdain the formalism, pomp and circumstance of the hierarchy (p. 52). From the same evidence the two groups were able to draw different conclusions and saw the same structure differently. Perhaps their answer is to be found 'in the web of interpersonal relationships in which these people were situated, in the past as well as in the present' (p. 53), so that the same Church comes to be differently evaluated by the two groups. Kotre suggests that the problems are to be resolved by 'getting at the starting points that shape individuals' conceptions of "what it's all about"' (p. 176). This of course is a confession that the problems of what makes a person move towards (or away from) philosophical, political and religious ideas have been too hard to deal with so far, except for the minor consistencies that are explained by the conditions of social learning or by their compatability with cultural expectations.

Although experimental studies of attitude change have assessed the effects of separate variables, social influence and decision-making in real situations show multiple effects. Conversions, whether religious or political, may be either gradual or sudden, but they reflect the continuous restructuring or realignment of cognitive elements that all but the most rigid show. Influence, relationships, dominance and control constitute a syndrome of social effects, but how do people come within the range of these influences? Personality effects in persuasibility or conformity, and cognitive processes in levelling–sharpening, in a search for knowledge or to achieve consistency may help to give explanations. Gamson and Modigliani (1966) observed that 'poorly informed individuals, even with different ideological orientations, will have difficulty relating their orientation to specific policies.' Campbell *et al.* (1960) noted the importance of a 'conceptual ability to participate in national policies'. They found that political (and religious) positions are mediated through families and other personal influences. These influences not only ensure the stability of voting behaviour but can also account for the fact that an absolute minority has any detailed knowledge of recognized ideologies.

The world view of the 'rational man' is a creation of ideologies, yet such a man's awareness and maturity is supposed to result in his emancipation from the processes that distort 'social reality'. The source of these distorting effects is in various personality processes. One view about ideology therefore involves its social bases, and refers to social realities and to social control and influence. Another view invokes concepts about rationalizing, intellectualizing, expressiveness and the other affective processes. The social view links to a sociology of knowledge. Mannheim's clarification of the 'relations between knowledge and social structure which had hitherto remained obscure' (Merton, 1968, p. 562) contrasts against the broad view of Freud who argued that those ideas survive which express and satisfy underlying psychic processes and pathologies.

Social constraints undoubtedly influence our construction of the world and are also a primary limitation on the unfettered expression of personality needs in any ideology. A lower-class black and a successful surgeon are subject to quite different constraints and experiences. Nevertheless social ideologies have themselves led to a recognition of the important place that individual or personality factors occupy in controlling and contributing to the shape of behaviour, especially in the bigoted adherence to particular views. These can be forced by situational constraints, by a public commitment, or by personality processes like rigidity. The possibility must be considered that an interpretation in terms of one of the conventional personality theories in fact uses an ideologically based and prior theory about personality and *its* effects. Some traits of personality have been found to be specific to situations (rather than to persons), or to the ways that subjects decide to present themselves publicly. Further work is needed to differentiate between the trait and other theories of personality, and those that emphasize the situation-specific nature of consistent behaviour (Argyle and Little, 1972). This last view also relates to the widely recognized consistency and dissonance theories that attribute ideological consistency to a need that individuals have to maintain stable relationships between the elements of cognition, feeling and behaviour. One way of resolving belief dilemmas is a failure to recognize the agreed or accepted ideological processes and content. It is always necessary to establish whether a readiness to respond depends on the logic of a belief system and an understanding of it, or on a tendency towards habitual styles of response independently of any specific content.

Gilbert and Levinson in their study of ideology, personality and institutional policy in mental hospitals in 1953, asked several questions including 'Do homogeneous systems recruit individuals whose personalities are receptive (or congruent) to the structurally required ideology?' 'Do systems change the initially unreceptive personalities?' and 'Can incongruent members change the system?' These questions are still to be properly answered. In their search for answers, some investigators have preferred to rely on grouped data from well-selected samples of subjects, while others have relied on their observation of one or of a few individuals.

Eysenck's dimensional theory

In any ideology it is possible to distinguish between the content (or what is to be believed) and the strength of adherence to the beliefs (or how fanatical believers can or must be). This distinction between content and structure has penetrated many psychological studies of ideology. For this reason there is a conflict, for example, between an authoritarian or a democratic orientation as adherence to specified doctrines and as a stance that involves either intolerance or tolerance, as a personality trait or an attitudinal disposition.

Many personality, attitude and belief scales have been factor analysed to establish the underlying patterns. These analyses deal with the items themselves or with the scores from several scales (depending to some extent on the computing facilities available). Although factor analysis is a complex statistical procedure, it is a simple operation with a computer: its purpose is to describe the relationships between separate elements, or to provide a kind of map that shows 'distances' (as 'loadings') over a more or less arbitarily defined 'factor space'.

Morris and Jones (1955) factored a 'ways to live' questionnaire across five cultures and found broadly similar dimensions in each. They describe five main factors covering social restraint and self-control, enjoyment in action, withdrawal and self-sufficiency, receptivity and sympathetic concern, and self-indulgence. These dimensions are essentially content-defined.

Eysenck (1954) analysed the organization of social attitudes and has reported some more recent results in a 1971 paper. Criticisms of the initial work have already been noted (page 46). His items covered a wide range and he found two main orthogonal factors, called T or the tough-mindedness-tendermindedness factor after the distinction that William James had drawn in 1907, and R or radicalism–conservatism. The axes in the first analysis were drawn in such a way that the item clusters fell in the quadrants between them, and were identified through allegiance to the main political positions. Thus fascists are tough-minded conservatives and communists are tough-minded radicals. Some argued that Ferguson's (1939) distinction between religionism and humanitarianism which entails a 45° rotation of the axes that Eysenck defined is a better solution (Christie, 1956a; Green and Stacey, 1964). Defining the dimensions is a general problem, found also in the analysis of religious material. The actual item content plays an important role in determining the dimensional patterns that are identified, as do the subjects who are used. The arguments relating to the dimensionality of religion have been traversed by Dittes (1969) and he says,

Theoretical concerns and general sophisticated reflection (either theological or psychological) seem to offer compelling arguments for multi-dimensionality. . . . Religion seems far too complex an area of human behaviour not to include many different and unrelated types of variables. Yet the net impact of much empirical work seems to suggest that, over fairly heterogeneous samples and using a variety of types of items, persons in a general population do tend to identify a common factor of religion or religiousness or religiosity' (p. 618).

We might repeat that a single factor emerges consistently from empirical analyses of specifically religious beliefs, and related social attitudes (cf. Brown, 1966). A further important distinction in studies of dimensionality must be made between the results obtained empirically and the theoretical reflection on the material that is being analysed.

To return to Eysenck's recent study (1971). He had twenty-eight items answered by a random sample of the adult population in Britain, and the following eight primary factors emerged: authoritarianism, religion, ethnocentrism, humanitarianism, sexual morale, tough-mindedness, age and sex. These are not independent or orthogonal factors, but they yielded two higher order orthogonal factors that were, as in the 1954 analysis, unrelated to social class. Factor 1 opposes authoritarianism and humanitarianism, and the second factor of religionism opposes religious belief and sexual permissiveness. These factors are aligned with the earlier R (radicalism) and T (tough-mindedness) factors, so that religious beliefs appear in the tender-minded conservative quadrant, authoritarian beliefs are in the tough-minded conservative quadrant, and so on. Expressed in this way the results align with Ferguson's distinction between religionism and humanitarianism (see Figure 2).

Eysenck argues that 'there is in truth only one ideological factor present in the attitude field, namely radicalism–conservatism' (1954, p. 170). He chose the dimensional name 'radical–conservative' to identify it because it has 'been used for centuries to organize and conceptualize groups of attitudes', and is a 'genuine social attitude factor'. The tough- and tender-minded dimension is interpreted not as 'an alternative ideological system' (p. 170), but as a projection on to the attitude field of extroverted and introverted personality patterns, with extroverts being tough and introverts tender in their expressions of radical or conservative attitudes.

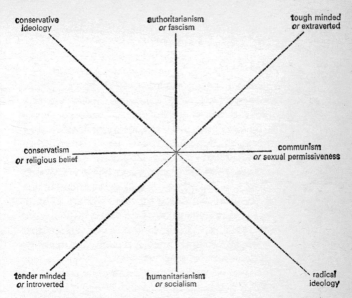

Figure 2 The structure of attitudes, following Eysenck, and others

An attractive aspect of Eysenck's theory is the extent to which it provides a link between attitude structures and their content, the conditions under which attitudes are acquired, and traits of temperament. The tough minded, being extraverted, are for the immediate gratification of aggressive and sexual impulses, and the tender minded are more concerned with ethical and religious ideas as barriers to satisfaction, from which Eysenck predicted that 'we should expect the "under-socialized" working class to be relatively tough-minded and the "over-socialized" middle class to be tender-minded' (1954, p. 299). The origins are to be found in differences in conditionability during the period of socialization so that the 'person showing high conditionability' becomes 'over-socialized'. His recent results do not in fact show class-based differences, and it seems somewhat ideological to expect them to occur. But a theory that allows one to move directly between

forms of socialization, personality characteristics and the
attitudes both of parents and their children has considerable
strength.

Other dimensions

Some other factors have been isolated, either theoretically or
empirically. Christie (1956a), in criticizing Eysenck's earlier
work argues for a means–end factor in ideologies. Yet such a
factor seems to have been primarily identified theoretically,
and is reminiscent of Parsons and Shils' very comprehensive
analysis of values (1951) and of Rokeach's (1970) value
classification. Kluckhohn (in Parsons and Shils, 1951) notes
'that the means–end dichotomy is not as clear-cut in the
category systems of all cultures as it is in Western culture'
(1951, p. 413). In considering values, Kluckhohn distinguished
dimensions of modality (positive and negative), content
(aesthetic, cognitive and moral), intent, generality and intensity,
explicitness, extent (in the sense of spread 'from a single
individual to the whole of humanity') and organization. An
example of another classificatory system is Whiting's analysis
of the five drive systems: oral, anal, sexual, defense, aggression.
Other systems have been proposed for their analytical convenience. Harris (1971) identified, largely on the basis of
content, cultural factors, traditional factors, conservatism east
and west, and nationalism. Scott (1969) deals with the contents
of cognitions through concepts, beliefs, attitudes, values and
so on. He has developed both a model and a set of techniques
to assess the structure of 'natural cognitions' conceived as the
ideas about objects and events that are entertained in the
absence of experimental intervention. This model can be
applied to define the static properties of a developed cognitive
system and covers dimensionality, articulation (the number of
distinctions that can be reliably made on a particular attribute),
evaluative centrality and cognitive integration. He reports a
validation in which maladjusted groups showed higher
ambivalence to others than did normal groups. In general he
found that more information increases the dimensionality of a
domain. A core of Scott's approach involves the use of several

methods to explore a single domain like nationalism, including checklists, paired comparisons, free descriptions, ratings and a similarities analysis (see page 29).

Within the specific context of ideologies most interest has been given to the patterns formed by their content and to the general relationships between attitudes and personality through concepts like 'dogmatism', and conservatism. Tomkins (1963), in an essay on 'Left and right: a basic dimension of ideology and personality', writes of 'the engagement of belief and feeling by ideology, when the ideo-affective postures are sufficiently similar to the ideological posture so that they reinforce and strengthen each other' (p. 389). He is specially concerned with the basic similarities between ideology as a social object or system and the responses that are made to it. Thus families of feelings and families of ideas become organized together, and the evaluation of an object becomes a part of the object itself. Tomkins identifies the posture and responses to romanticism in literature as similar to that to revolution in politics. He says these 'resonances' reflect the prevailing and available ideologies. Familiarity with historical processes is to Tomkins a prerequisite for the development of an ideological posture – although he also says that it should be possible to predict the postures to which individuals will resonate when making predictions across domains. He proceeds to identify bi-polarities in mathematics, in the philosophy of science, in metaphysics, epistemology, and ethics between the forms of realism and of idealism. Tomkins catalogues other differences, as between love and control in child-rearing, and in art and music. He summarizes these abstractions by relating them to man as, or as not, an end in himself – so that beliefs about man become the fundamental question, to which there are answers possible at many levels. A common bond between all ideologies is to be found in their concern with aspects of the human condition.

We seem to have a facility or perhaps a tendency to organize our cognitions and/or awareness, and to simplify and classify our knowledge and experience. In this way complex issues are simplified and organized into patterns. Butler and Stokes (1969, pp. 212–13), using a Left–Right dichotomy as the framework for interpreting change in political attitudes concluded that 'Consistencies are higher for those with a well-elaborated or interpreted ideological awareness, in the particular case considered, along a Left–Right dimension'. Some patterns of organization are imposed when knowledge is acquired initially, and others are constructed by each person for himself, perhaps to conform with a rage for order or consistency. Any resolution of the questions about dimensionality in attitudes and about the personality processes involved will depend on the responses that an individual makes to the ideas and ideals that are available to him, and to his resolution of the strains both towards and against consistency in them.

There are many possible applications or projections of these distinctions. One important set is to be found in the ways behaviour is analysed implicitly, especially in relation to its control, to feelings and other emotional responses. Tomkins has identified ten specific polarities, as between tolerance and intolerance, between maximizing affect and maximizing normative behaviour, and between pluralism and hierarchy in an individual's feelings. (Distinctions between tolerance and intolerance in primary human affect and experience can either be projected on to social situations or applied to individuals.) The main alternatives to such structured analyses throws attention to the dynamics of the behaviour of individuals as an ongoing process.

9 Ideologues and True Believers

In examining any general personality involvements in ideology, the variables or traits that are usually identified entail social components, and the typical research design summarizes the data from a number of subjects. Therefore the emphasis in the previous chapter was more on followers than on their leaders. But an analysis of group trends is unlikely to achieve the refinement needed to predict the effects on, or the responses of, single individuals.

Two kinds of study have been more specifically concerned with individuals. One collects contemporary material from 'ordinary people', with the results described rather anonymously. The other method involves some interpretation of whatever data are already available about historically important figures. The many pitfalls and the benefits of using personal documents to build a psychological account were traversed by Allport in 1942.

Interviews

In Adorno *et al.* (1950), the detailed case studies of Larry and Mack are given as typical of low and high authoritarians. Smith, Bruner and White (1956) used several techniques of personality measurement and interviewing to describe in detail the attitudes of ten men towards the Soviet Union. Their subjects were drawn from different walks of life and each was seen for two hours a week for fifteen weeks. All but one of them were hostile to the Soviet regime; social experiences and personality dynamics are described that had shaped the complex inner content of their attitudes, which in turn expressed and confirmed the social and psychic forces that had generated them. It was concluded that the detailed structure of these attitudes had been selectively fashioned to reflect each person's individuality, and that the same expressed attitude functioned differently from one person to another. In their analysis, attitudes are described as a resultant or compromise between reality demands, social demands and inner psychological demands. These three factors are said to be inseparable, and the authors warn against giving undue stress to any one, asserting that emphasis on reality demands alone led to the rationalism common in the nineteenth century. Emphasis on social factors leads to a passive conception of the individual, and 'emphasis on externalization alone is the route to the kind of irrationalism that marked the earliest impact of the psycho-analytic movement' (p. 275). Social attitudes are also influenced by available information, by intellectual ability and by the individual's own style. Multiple determination operates in both the expressive, and the adjustive or instrumental forms of attitudes, and Smith, Bruner and White stress that there is 'no rigid or one-to-one relationship between the opinions a person develops and the underlying needs or dynamics of his personality' (p. 278). Throughout their discussion, they stress the differences between people in the meaning and in the structure of their attitudes.

Lengthy interviews were carried out by Almond (1954) with defectors from communism. He incidentally reports that only 27 per cent of his subjects had been exposed to communist literature before joining the party. Lane (1962) interviewed fifteen working-class men and found that they did not contextualize their political beliefs and had a low level of information about them. Bettelheim and Janowitz (1950) carried out an 'in-depth' study of the prejudices of veterans, and Riesman derived his description of three forms of social character as inner-, outer-, and other-directed from the interviews that are described in *Faces in the Crowd* (1952). Davies (1966) reports on the political beliefs of a number of Australians.

The first part of Keniston (1960) reports the results of an intensive interview method, supplemented by a systematic use of psychometric tests. He worked closely with twelve alienated students for three years and also investigated twelve unalienated and another twelve control subjects. The broad aim was to describe the psychology of alienation and in the second part of his book he deals with the alienating society. He notes that there is substantial philosophical support for many alienated views (p. 82) as well as a rhetoric for it (p. 453) and he distinguishes those who cannot help being alienated from those who 'choose to be alienated'.

These interview studies raise a question of the contrast between the depth and detail of an interview and the complexity of the material that can be elicited there, against the simplicity of data based on sets of closed questions answered by large, controlled samples of subjects. Well-recognized difficulties of any interview method include the implicit demands that are imposed by the interviewer on his subjects, the intrusion of implicit personality theories, and the difficulties of adequately summarizing and ordering the material that has been collected to allow more than just a description of the subjects' characteristics.

Interviews may be improved if they are guided by an explicit theory. It is therefore necessary to find a model that allows a categorization of the phenomena and their interrelationships, that indicates the appropriate analytic units to be employed, and that provides a language with which to describe and compare the phenomena (Jones, 1971). Kelly's construct theory has been proposed as such a model. It has the advantage of dealing with the kinds of verbal material on which clinicians must typically rely, using as a method the repertory grid (Bannister and Mair, 1968). Alternatively, the model of Miller, Galanter and Pribram (1960) treats the critical elements of behaviour as a man's image or internal cognitive representation of himself and his world, and of the plans that he sets out to execute in it. Jones notes that individuals function in three interrelated realms: the biological, the social and the important realm that is organized around a 'sense of personal identity and reflected in his value system and personal ideology' (1971). A further model holds that ideological (and other) behaviour is always driven and formed by primitive and unconscious processes. These processes explain complex adult behaviour by identifying the elementary form of which a person himself may be unaware. Each of these models would be expected to use its own peculiar data.

An entirely different approach is to be found in Klapp's (1968) analysis of the public, external character of popular leaders like explorers and film stars. He used drama and the theatre as a basis for analysing the roles and the problems confronted by a 'symbolic leader', 'who functions primarily through his meaning or image' (p. 7) when he is cast in a certain defined role by his audience.

Clinical approaches

An adaptation of the interview method was used by Rokeach (1964) when he examined changes in the delusional belief systems of three men who claimed the same identity, each believing himself to be Christ. The interaction of these men on a hospital ward over a period of six months was observed and detailed background material was gathered about each one. It is suggested in the conclusion that each man had discarded his original identity and suffered paranoid delusions of grandeur as a defence against confusion about his sexual identity, tinged for two with a sense of shame over feelings of incompetence as a male, and for the third with 'guilt about forbidden sexual and aggressive impulses' (pp. 326–7). These responses are discussed in the context of each man's early life, and the coherent threads in their development are outlined.

Rokeach has also developed a classification of terminal and instrumental values and applied it in a content analysis of values that underlie political writings. In one study (1970) this method was applied to the twelve Federalist papers written between 1787 and 1788 that are of disputed authorship. With judgements made over twenty-four values, it was found that these papers are closer to the style of Madison in the papers of known authorship than to that of Hamilton. Content analysis using the General Inquirer has similarly been used to describe some of the patterns implicit in a person's style of ideological expression (cf. the analysis of the 'Letters from Jenny', Paige, 1965).

It seems to be widely assumed that the aim of a psychological analysis is to use information about the early formative years of a person's life to understand and explain the subsequent events. This view derives from psychoanalytic theory, and contrasts with the view that a conscious striving after meaning, order and consistency sustains a person's identity and the continuities in his behaviour. Freud himself applied his psychoanalytic theory to the lives of historically important figures. His first psychoanalytic biography was a study of the life and personality of Leonardo da Vinci in which he deals with the significance of Leonardo's emotional and sexual life and his fantasies relating to his 'double nature as an artist and as a scientific investigator' (1910/1963, p. 105). In this essay, Freud also considered the problems of writing any biography. He said that

Biographers are fixated on their heroes in a quite special way. In many cases they have chosen their hero as the subject of their studies because – for reasons of their personal emotional life – they have felt a special affection for him from the very first. They then devote their energies to a task of idealization, aimed at enrolling the great man among the class of their infantile models – at reviving in him, perhaps, the child's idea of his father. To gratify this wish they obliterate the individual features of their subject's physiognomy; they smooth over the traces of his life's struggles with internal and external resistances, and they tolerate in him no vestige of human weakness or imperfection. They thus present us with what is in fact a cold, strange, ideal figure, instead of a human being to whom we might feel ourselves distantly related. That they should do this is regrettable, for they thereby sacrifice truth to an illusion, and for the sake of their infantile fantasies abandon the opportunity of penetrating the most fascinating secrets of human nature (1910, pp. 177–8; on pages 183–4 Freud discusses other limitations on this method of building a biography).

Political and religious figures have been subjected to a similar analysis. Freud wrote about Moses. Ludwig Jekels wrote 'The turning point in the life of Napoleon I' in 1914. This is said to be the first attempt to use psychoanalytic understanding to solve an historical problem, in this case why Napoleon became a French Patriot (see Schmidl, 1962). Much of Jekels' analysis concerned family relationships, with interpretive equations like 'the fatherland is a cover representation for the mother'. Despite the sparseness of the material available, Jekels's interpretation rests on the oedipus complex, but as Schmidl notes, 'this phenomenon is too universal to be used for interpretation of a historical vicissitude.' Ernest Jones also wrote about Napoleon, and Lean (1970) has recently described some characteristics of those in England who were admirers of Napoleon, and who seem to have shared a similar formation of attitudes and character in childhood.

Psycho-biography

Erikson has stressed the importance of a clinician's training in allowing him to recognize major trends when all the facts are not available and to make predictions about what might prove to have happened. He argues that the validity of a theme in biography depends on its crucial recurrence during a person's development. Clinical methods employ highly sophisticated techniques of interviewing and emphasize the 'patient's latent embeddedness in his milieu, with which he is in both conscious and unconscious interaction. The clinical method identifies implicit meanings and may give quite novel perspectives on the data. To modify the method and to apply a dynamic theory to second-hand material about a subject rather than to the subject himself can present difficulties. But this is what a psycho-biography involves, and Erikson has refined and developed this method to a fine tool. In his study of *Young Man Luther* (1959), he relies on three crucial occurrences in the young Luther's life: the vow to become a monk, made during a thunderstorm; the fit in the choir at Erfurt in which he raved 'It isn't me!'; and the experience in the tower of the monastery in Wittenburg when he felt himself to be reborn. Erikson interprets these events within his theory of identity development. Evidence is introduced about Luther's conflicts with his father, and his conflict between his father on earth and the father in heaven. So Luther's theological system is treated as a psychological datum that is need determined, conflict laden, symptomatic, wish-fulfilling and thematically consistent with his dominant personal concerns. But the analysis is not a negative one, because in acting out his own conflicts Luther detonated social forces that led to enormously creative reforms in Europe. (There are extended reviews of *Young Man Luther* by a political scientist, L. W. Pye, and psychoanalyst, D. de Bols, in Marvick (1961).)

Erikson's theory of identity development specifies eight stages in the life-cycle, each based in different social relationships: so the first requires the resolution of basic social trust against mistrust. A later stage of 'identity versus role confusion' involves a search for social values that will form an identity as a 'defined world image' (1950/1965, p. 254). Erikson (1950/1965) stresses the universal processes that can be recognized in individuals, as well as the underlying equivalences between, for example, sadistic perversions and forms of religious piety. Defence mechanisms give the key to specified equivalences, since their purpose is to safeguard the ego and to ward off the extremes of the id and the super-ego. As Erikson put it, 'The ego, then, is an "inner institution" evolved to safeguard that order within individuals on which all order depends' (1950/1965, p. 188). Political leaders and nations (at another level) are especially involved in the search for an identity. National processes although collective have been described in (macro-) psychological terms. So Erikson applied his theory to Hitler and to the German people as a whole. Hitler's pathologies have been frequently diagnosed, but as Erikson says, 'On the stage of German history, Hitler sensed to what extent it was safe to let his own personality represent with hysterical abandon what was alive in every German listener and reader. Thus the role he chose reveals as much about his audience as about himself . . .' (1950/1965, p. 321). Responses towards leaders have offered a continuing problem for analysis: some resolutions of this issue have been in terms of similarities in modal personality processes, a symbolic equivalence between leader and led, and the simple acceptance of appeals as guiding images. But Erikson stresses the 'recognition of the obvious fact' that spheres of exploitation are 'matters pertaining to the social process and not in themselves to be explained as originating in infantile anxiety' (p. 396).

Any leader or ideologue must reconcile his own needs with the social pressures, if he is to succeed and have an effect. It is hard to establish whether the ideological leaders who have changed history first aspired to power and then faced their difficulties, or whether they had first to confront their own problems. Most have had to deal with problems stemming from the fact that ideological leaders are much sought after.

Autobiography

We cannot offer a general explanation of the ways in which ideologues are built, except in the few outstanding cases that seem to have showed rather clear influences. Although the lives of many have invited interpretation, the quality of the information that is available imposes limits on these interpretations. Whether the material comes from autobiography, biography or from some kind of hagiography, it may be more important as a political or religious document or as a statement of ideology than as data for a psychological analysis of the subject himself. To treat such documents as a valid personal statement or analogous to a case history may be too naive, and not only because of distorted memories or a deliberate reshaping. Thus Erikson described Gandhi's autobiography, published in weekly instalments in an Indian newspaper, as a cautionary tale meant to advise and guide young men, 'for the purpose of recreating oneself in the image of one's own method; and ... to make that image convincing' (quoted by Rudolph and Rudolph, 1967, p. 170). The Rudolphs note that Gandhi's autobiography

must be read with a particularly sensitive ear, one that hears what he has to say concerning his diet, or his relations to his wife, and considers what it might mean for his political style and for how that style was received. To relegate these remarks to the category of personal frills and curiosities that constitute the gossip rather than the serious significance of a great man is to miss what was central to his leadership (1967, p. 171).

As the Rudolphs also noted, 'Confessions are acceptable in saints, like Augustine, or in professional sensualists, like de

Sade, or understandable in a tortured exhibitionist, like Rousseau. But in a political man?' (p. 169).

In *Gandhi's Truth*, Erikson (1970) describes how the material for this psycho-biography was gathered from documents, and from people who had themselves been close to Gandhi. Erikson says he found similarities between Gandhi and Freud, and in Gandhi he rediscovered 'psychoanalysis in terms of truth, self-sufficiency and non-violence' (1970, p. 439). Significant events that invited psychological interpretation were Gandhi's sexual behaviour and attitudes, and the feminine identification that was related to his commitment to non-violence and to truth. But lives *usually* involve an organized pattern, especially in retrospect. So Rudolph and Rudolph can easily say that Gandhi's ideas and techniques were restatements of the truths he learned in his childhood (1967, p. 247).

A further example of the application of an underlying psychic determinism is to be found in Bakan's (1965) treatment of Augustine, whose attachment to his mother was said to be expressed symbolically in the fact that he described his mother's death in the ninth book of his *Confessions*. Augustine's identification with Jesus is seen by the fact that he was thirty-three at his conversion. This interpretation by Bakan is one of a set of six which employ different approaches to the psycho-biography of St Augustine. Religious movements are always closely associated with accounts and disclosures about their leaders, with the Gospels a leading example. The detailed psychological interpretation of these accounts is a post-Freudian phenomenon, but as Woolcott (1966) says, 'To determine from his life a great man's psychopathology is easy – it is usually glaring. To determine the development of his genius, there is the rub. Psychological studies of great men suggest that they achieve their greatness because of and in spite of intense conflict.' In his discussion of Augustine, Dittes speaks of providing the spectacles through which Augustine looked on the world, and he describes his task as specifying the correspondence or consistency between ideology and character, and between thought and life. But the circumstances of

Augustine's birth and his early life are assumed to be quite critical for all these analyses.

Although not autobiographical, films, novels and plays are important in giving direction to some social movements, and their authors cannot be disregarded. So Parkin (1968, p. 99 ff.) lists the novelists, artists, dramatists and actors who supported the Campaign for Nuclear Disarmament and notes the absence of scientists. Similar influences could be detected in regard to the movements surrounding the Vietnam War, or Black Power in the United States.

Diagnosis

An alternative to some psychodynamic interpretation is a frankly psychiatric approach. A recent example is Storr's study of Churchill, in which he diagnosed 'cyclothymic temperament, with a pronounced tendency to depression' (1969, p. 215). Storr makes reference to Churchill's physique, and to the familial evidence for a constitutional basis for his depression. He quotes Lord Moran's comment about Churchill's 'inner world of make believe': 'In 1940 his inner world of make believe coincided with the facts of external reality in a way which rarely happens to any man' (p. 245). He is said to have been the right kind of leader when England 'needed a prophet, a heroic visionary, a man who could dream dreams of victory when all seemed lost.' Churchill emerges as a man of action and of power, and not as an ideologue. His undoubted influence shows that different kinds of leaders are needed for the necessarily diverse roles, while Storr observes that psycho-analytic insight is inadequate 'to explain Churchill's remarkable courage'.

Generalizations

A general integration of private psychopathological motiva-tions and public political acts was made by Lasswell (1930). Money-Kyrle applied the concepts of projection and defence, the oedipus complex and the super-ego to political behaviour. He writes that, 'one defence against depression seems to be of such over-riding political significance that it deserves to be singled out for a separate treatment. . . . The experience is the almost accidental discovery of the clinical importance of certain beliefs, usually of a religious or philosophical nature, which a patient has hitherto belittled rather than concealed' (1951, p. 173). But he goes on to note that 'When "a system" appears as an ideology common to a sect or party, there will be many in whom it is accepted more as a convention than because it has any great psychological importance to them' (p. 176). Here is the problem of generalization again, and separate paths to an ideology, or to a point of view must be recognized. They will include conversion, reasoning, and some direct social influence that presupposes bonds of attraction, knowledge and prior experience. Yet the possibility remains that personality processes may override both the cognitive and the social control of belief states. This is certainly Lasswell's approach: 'Our general theory of the political man stressed three terms, the private motives, their displacement on to public objects and their rationalization in terms of public interest. The agitator values mass-response (and is) strongly narcissistic' (1930, p. 124).

Although personal or case histories can clarify some aspects of ideological involvement, the detection of patterns in them involves selecting material and making an extrapolation. The most general conclusions are that life events and experiences are important in forming ideologies, and that social situations facilitate the expression of personality processes. Yet a life history may itself be a kind of myth since in most people's lives fact and illusion are interchangeable. In Levi-Strauss' use, a myth is a sequence that belongs to the past, but it is also a pattern that can be detected and used in the present. It is a double structure, historical and ahistorical. Edelson writes of the 'patient's personal myth' (1971, p. 58) as itself an explanation, and Allport continually emphasized the fact that contemporary events give more information than does a reconstruction of long-forgotten or half-remembered experiences. To peel back the layers of motivation and meaning may involve explanations only by 'explaining away', and although the reasons for a particular stance may differ from person to person, their social effects may be very similar, and similar 'reasons' can produce different forms of social behaviour. Not too many have been able to act out their conflicts (if that is what Luther, Cromwell and the rest were doing), or have been able to express their pathologies publicly. Few are like the political assassins who, almost of necessity, have had their behaviour subjected to a close public scrutiny (Weisz and Taylor, 1969) (so Lincoln's assassin is thought to have made a paranoid response because he unconsciously substituted Lincoln for his own brother).

While specific motivations may be identified in some extreme cases, they are usually deeply embedded in philosophical, ideological or religious positions. Perhaps, as Erikson suggests, the well adjusted don't ask metaphysical questions, or to follow Godin (1964), some religious beliefs are expressions of ego-centricity and immaturity, and a believer must strive to decentre and 'purify his image of God' to relieve their immaturities. The really influential people have been able to transform both themselves and their world.

Commitment to an ideology may occupy a central place in a person's identity. This chapter has considered some of the studies which have tried to clarify what individuals have been on about, and to establish whether knowledge of their lives can make their beliefs more (or less) credible. The broad hypothesis specifies an articulation of a person's belief and knowledge of the world with social events and institutions, and with the norms and values that are linked to personality. It is no novelty to argue that a person's view of the way the world is constructed involves integrated responses and is linked with other events. Horowitz (in Waxman 1969, p. 166) quoted Pangloss's remarks to Candide:

All events are linked up in this best of all possible worlds; for, if you had not been expelled from the noble castle by hard kicks in your backside for love of Mademoiselle Cunegoide, if you had not been clamped into the Inquisition, if you had not wandered about America on foot, if you had not stuck your sword into the Baron, if you had not lost all your sheep from the land of Eldorado, you would not be eating candied citrons and pistachios here.

The novelty is to be found rather in an examination of intra-psychic conflicts, or at least in a man's psychological background and development, and we now have a rich vocabulary for these effects. Information about outside events becomes interpreted in terms of internal processes, and delusions and projections, rationalizations and conflicts, dependence and autonomy, ambivalence and phantasy, and character types are readily available concepts. The 'facts' of a biography are then a complex blend of a person's account of his own situation and the (perhaps) thinly concealed characteristics that are obvious to detached observers or to clinicians. Strachey says that the biographer 'will attack his subject in unexpected places. . . . He will row out over that great ocean of material, and lower down into it, here and there, a little bucket, which will bring up to the light of day some characteristic specimen, from those far depths, to be examined with a careful curiosity' (1921, p. vii). This process is necessarily guided by theory, and by standard interpretations.

10 And in Conclusion: a Synthesis

Social psychology has developed with twin orientations: towards the behaviour of individuals, and towards the study of groups and social institutions. Many concepts involve one or other of these two points of view. So an ideology about authority, politics, sex or religion can be construed as a trait or characteristic of individuals, or as a kind of relationship that emerges between individuals. The psychological study of ideology rests on individual response, acceptance or adherence to ideas or beliefs about social issues, and on situationally or socially defined constraints or interpretations of behaviour. Both of these aspects involve responses that may give an affectively *or* cognitively based patterning to that behaviour which is defined as socially relevant. In oversimplified terms, a psychological analysis is expected to define 'who believes what ideologies, for which reasons, and with what consequences'.

Continued use of the concept of 'ideology' seems assured so long as social boundaries are drawn between groups and conflicts of interest remain a matter of concern. Although racial and physical characteristics may be more obvious than are the differences marked by holding religious or other beliefs, it is not new for an explicit recognition of social differences to be built on the basis of apparent or assumed opinions and beliefs. People's ideas then become labelled for them, and these labels have patent influences on social awareness and interaction. An ideology becomes a strong way of abstracting, conceptualizing and evaluating the social environment. One effect of this 'rage for order' is to provide relatively enduring social and intellectual structures to social interaction. The popular restriction of ideologies to politics, religion and sex is too limited.

Our focus in this book has been on individuals and their behavioural consistencies, and not on ideologies as philosophies or systems of ideas. Simple psychological explanations have been rejected. Any behaviour, whether it is social nudism or participation in a protest march, will be complexly motivated. It could reflect a simple preference just for that kind of behaviour, or might result from the acceptance of doctrines, ideals, or principles about such behaviour. Some psychologists have argued the principle that any doctrines will serve to rationalize behaviour and are necessarily derived from unconscious motives. Such reductionism is itself a kind of ideology. Interpreting and explaining the reasons for behaviour is obviously difficult, and whatever interpretations are offered reflect ideologies about what is involved. A preferable solution is to find or produce good and reliable evidence to support the validity of any interpretation. Motivational questions are more usually tested against clinical-type data than by using the 'objective' measures common in social-psychological studies. Whatever method is used will to some extent limit the conclusions that may be drawn.

Identification of the content of an ideology, whether in relation to an explicit formulation or from an analysis of what people believe is a first stage towards its measurement, and interviews are commonly used to define the details of a believed ideological system. The methods developed to study thought disorders could profitably be adapted to define linkages and consistencies in the elements of patterned beliefs, and in the knowledge of ideological material. Beyond the initial stages of any inquiry, developed scales and measures are used to explore adherence to the content and concepts of an ideology and the understanding of them. This material supports and embodies a recognized point of view that can align people with a social movement. Beliefs and group memberships can become institutionalized, and early zeal develop into a hollow routine. Extra-psychological influences, including political and economic conditions may also shape and limit behavioural expressions of underlying ideas.

Beyond the content of an ideology is its style or structure, and different forms of attachment to ideas and beliefs could depend on whether emotional, intellectual, habitual or social influences were predominant. The stability of widely accepted beliefs, and the complex support that is available for both actions and ideology mean that changes in belief usually occur slowly, and that beliefs do not have to have clear effects on actual behaviour. Contrasts between thought and action run through the theories about ideology, and echo Mannheim's (1936) distinction between ideology and utopia as the difference between what can *not* be implemented and that which can. The same contrast penetrates accounts of religious and political behaviour as well as the whole field of attitude theory, and might even be similar to the basic separation between introversion (with a predominance of thought) and extraversion (or action) as personality dispositions.

Many people search for some coherence in explanation and for an understanding of social processes. This search is especially obvious in the responses to disruptive social movements, and is satisfied by explanations in factual or historical assertions, or in credal, doctrinal or interpretive statements. Once achieved, the explanations tend to become highly stable. To observe that Northern Ireland is in turmoil, or that women are socially disadvantaged are factual statements that *may* also imply an ideological stance simply by being noted. To attribute these events to a class war, a communist plot, divine rulings or natural justice is certainly ideological. In a rather similar way, to work for a cause or to become involved in a protest might imply expectations about possible solutions, or it may merely be a consequence of adventitious pressures. Beliefs and actions do not necessarily correspond.

A psychological interest in ideologies arises from the fact that they involve people's response to, and ideas about, the social environment. All responses are influenced by previous experiences and the effects of socialization. They involve agreements and accepted emotional or evaluative assessments, although not among those who fail to recognize a particular issue. Although many of these responses will be covert, they can often be described introspectively and are certainly deduced from or attributed to the behaviour of others. Thoughts, feelings and actions become patterned, so that when a person reflects on the world and his place in it, he may develop a theory or a plan about it that becomes a practical guide for action.

Commitment to an explicit action, even if it is only to make counter-attitudinal arguments, is a stronger way of binding responses than is a passive assent to statements of attitude or belief (cf. Kiesler, 1971). Attitudes are held more strongly when some action is elicited than if they are merely thought about or reflected on. And so some organizations insist on active proselytizing by their members.

Some generalizations

An ideology gives answers to important questions and defines approaches to them. Individuals differ in the strength of their acceptance of ideological material, and groups and movements differ in the ways in which their doctrines and the expected acceptance of them intersect. Although the concept of a 'thought crime' may be recent, overt conformity to a set of doctrines with 'mental reservation' is not new in either political or religious groups. Furthermore, explanations of behaviour often contrast 'external reasons' (like social pressures, drunkenness or stupidity) against a more internal justification that refers to the attitudes or motives involved. In many social movements, only a minority appear to be strongly committed. It is rather curious that psychologists took so long to recognize (perhaps because of their prior assumptions) that the situational demands on a person impose biases on his behaviour and so influence the outcome of any measures. While agreement is needed about the measures that can be properly made, it is 'Mannheim's paradox' that, in pursuing truth, social scientists are handicapped by their narrow focus and by distortions implicit in their own scientific (and other) ideologies.

Radical critics of the social sciences have claimed that the established theories and methods in psychology are conformist, Procrustean and Western, and that they simply attribute to error many important effects that don't fit with accepted, yet ideologically based, theories. The alternative theories are just as committed ideologically and *some* 'scientific' justification can be found for most social trends, somewhere in the sciences of human behaviour (this point is referred to by Ehrlich, 1971). The personal and social background of any investigator or theorist, and the extra-scientific influences on him may therefore throw the problems that he decides to take up into a roughly predictable mould. In their common traditions social psychologists are now more oriented to questions about structure than to an examination of the detailed and specific content of a problem. Perhaps as psychologists we need to take a step back to look again at actual processes and events and to reconstruct our explanations of their effects. There is no other empirical procedure for understanding why people differ in their orientations to thought or action, in their preferences for inner or outer forms of control, or in their use of explanations that rest on public events or on private experience.

An ideology involves commitment to a recognized position. Strongly held beliefs create a reality, but they can also limit and become a straitjacket of paranoid or obsessive responses. These effects are to be seen in some reactions to communism, socialism or catholicism, and the more extremely, rigidly or vigorously that beliefs are held, the more they seem to have invited interpretation, whether on psychological, sociological or other grounds. A public and explicit commitment to an ideology can force role-related behaviours which suppress idiosyncracies. So clergymen, lawyers, or party members are under pressure to think and act consistently and ideologically, and their behaviour reinforces and justifies their beliefs. Ideologies also become embedded in communities and cultures and are preserved by the acknowledged leaders, while those who do not hold an ideology are labelled as alienated. Words like fanatic, agnostic and apostate refer to other modes of adherence. That such words were originally applied in religious contexts suggests that different states of mind about belief have long been recognized.

Ideologies are concepts and cognitive awareness shapes an individual's responses to his culture, which in turn explains and controls aspects of behaviour. Unconscious components in stable beliefs and attitudes are a focus in theories of a personality-based support for social behaviour, a view also to be found in the functional analyses of attitudes. The cognitive consistency models, with an algebra of attitude change, predict relationships between valued objects and give a different key with which to understand the attachments to beliefs and attitudes. In these theories, a person's behaviour helps to make compossible the weights or values attached to specific objects or issues. These may be derived in their turn from a more general orientation or predisposition. The basis of a person's attitudes (and knowledge) will be a mix of half-forgotten material, and of organized and over-generalized experiences. Opinions may be a reaction against a particular context, as can be seen among those who have 'dropped-out' of the patterns expected by parents or others in authority, although they may reflect cognitive and emotional rigidity, or a low tolerance for novelty and change. Other theories define attitudes as a balance between inner and outer control, between field dependence and independence or between pervasive styles of response. Social influences, the ideological content itself, or wishes and feelings may each override any of the other factors. Once an ideology has been identified, whether as a result of specific training or because of a predisposition towards a particular style, the pattern of identification may change, while resistance to the recognition of an ideology is itself interpreted ideologically by some.

The realities of social and interpersonal conflicts based on reputed or assumed ideologies have made questions about the content of men's minds and about the ways in which they can be changed by persuasion, education, conversion, group loyalty, or indoctrination and 'brainwashing', of critical importance. Many social groups are identified either with or through their ideologies, so that Protestants value work, members of the middle class value security, and communists are subversive. Attitudes are predicted, and the predictability of the people one knows suggests intuitively that there are strong underlying patterns that influence their beliefs.

Ideologies are therefore sets of structures, preferences or dispositions that intersect. They involve many social situations and different kinds of content produce social awareness, so that detailed interpretations can explain specific responses. Individuals act in and through the institutional structures that force or carry systems of ideas and which involve the control of behaviour. Any social hierarchy ensures such control. Control in the Church is illustrated in Brecht's *Galileo*, when in Scene 12 Pope Urban VIII alters his expressed opinions from sympathy with Galileo to condemnation in the hands of the Inquisition as he vests to excommunicate him. The power inherent in some roles in a social structure reinforces the attitudes that are held or developed by the people who occupy these roles. The opportunities for an individual to change any movement or institution depend on the power available to him, and social behaviour is limited by the social norms and structure, and by the personalities of those involved. The details of these mechanisms of change are still poorly understood, despite the fact that some group effects are predictable.

Newcomb argued that 'individuals continually face a three-pronged problem of adaptation. Each of us must somehow come to terms, simultaneously, with the other individuals and groups of which our interpersonal environment is constituted, with the (social) world that we have in common with those persons and groups and with our own, intrapersonal autistic demands' (1961, p. 259). One function of ideology is to make available a system of explanation that provides a context within which social interaction can take place. In doing this, an ideology limits and restricts the possible forms of expression, and defines recognized values and orientations that can direct behaviour. Ideologies therefore have an important role in controlling social interaction because, of necessity, individuals must operate with limited repertoires of response.

Many ideological systems have a core with peripheral variants. The core is defined by a general content like economic determinism, or by a recognized orientation like tolerance or intolerance. The peripheral variants interpenetrate, and their similarities may link different systems. While a detailed ideological content can be explicitly formulated, individuals will differ in their sensitivity to or knowledge of it, perhaps because of conflicting interests and values or because of their prejudices. The coherence of an ideology appears to carry its own pressures towards enforced consistency. Ideologies, like social attitudes, are organized, and can be grouped along a dimension from liberal or radical to conservative. Many have argued that those with liberal attitudes are 'better', being more intelligent with a higher educational achievement, while the conservatives appear to show neurotic tendencies. So some people appear unable to engage in anything that resembles an ideological debate, whether because of its abstractness or because of their own rigidity. *The response to ideologies is therefore personal although their basis is social.*

Campbell (1960) found that in political behaviour only 11·5 per cent of a national US sample were aware of any ideological ground, and that 42 per cent voted according to a group benefit, 17·5 per cent voted irrelevantly to party issues, and the remainder fell into an intermediate category. The evidence about political behaviour that Sears (1969) has summarized leads to the conclusion that only a minority have stable attitudes backed by sound and accurate information. With religious material, Allport (1966) reported that about a quarter of his subjects were inconsistently pro-religious and agreed with all the religious items in his questionnaire, without regard to the detailed content. The ideologically committed may therefore be a knowledgeable minority, leaving the majority confused and ill-informed, or just not seeing the problem. But many are influenced by the available ideological positions. In a study of the effects of female ideology on the educational and occupational aspirations of the wives of American graduate students (Lipman-Blumen, 1972), it was found that the women who were informed and emancipated achieved more than did those with a traditional orientation. Other ideological positions can obscure some tendencies or facilitate the direct expression of fear or hostility, influence processes of socialization, or invite explanations in economic and political terms and Converse writes of the constraints and the articulation between idea-elements in belief systems and ideologies in emphasizing the differences between the sophistication of an elite, and the undifferentiated response of the mass 'public' (in Apter, 1964, p. 229).

There is ambiguity in the attachments to an ideology since some can tyrannize for an ideal that others would be prepared to die for. So ideologies may have effects on action. They can be reduced to a set of beliefs to which accepted tests of truth can be applied and are supported from psychologic and the other arguments assumed to be relevant. In Levinson's now quite old formulation, any individual selects or rejects his ideology from the range of defined alternatives available to him using the knowledge that is available. Some solutions will fit with his personality functions and at the same time satisfy social goals for instrumental or expressive purposes. So Levinson said (in his traditional family ideology paper in 1954) that 'A complete theory of ideology must take account of the interaction of intra-personal, specific situational and general sociocultural factors.' We cannot yet specify the relative contributions of these factors, despite the recent improvements in measurement and the now general awareness of ideologies. This awareness has allowed some decentration of beliefs and may even have reduced the possibilities of rationalization and the indirect expression of needs through ideological forms. All behaviours fit somewhere between the poles of social and personality-based origins or control.

Social pressures are generally strong, and the models available to any individual will influence his choice of ideologies and the strength of his attachment to them. Once an ideology has been accepted, its effects may spread to other areas and influence decisions about family size, voting behaviour or religious affiliation. These decisions are not *necessarily* made on ideological grounds, since they could be made on another basis or on none. But once an ideological base is exposed, its influences may be recognized and it can generalize to a guiding

principle and facilitate consistent responses. The effects of
ideologies are therefore tied closely to an awareness of them,
and to the concepts and the language used by them. A person's
awareness of an ideology may depend on his position in a
social structure, and certainly it reflects patterns of alignment,
involves authority and social influence, and the credibility of
information sources, although these may be more readily
accepted by 'convergent thinkers'. The effects cumulate and
ideologies can structure social events by identifying and giving
labels for the behaviour of others. Most of these effects are less
a question of some wished-for truth or 'need to believe' than a
necessary consequence of social influences operating on any
behaviour.

*An ideology about other ideologies itself becomes a structure
to which people can cling to interpret behaviour so it screens out
and simplifies the possible patterns of response.* Although an
ideology produces consistency, the wide differences between
individuals in its effects cannot be too heavily stressed.

Finally

Psychologically an ideology is a system of beliefs about social
issues, with strong effects in structuring thoughts, feelings and
behaviour. Information processing and decision making are
facilitated when established categories are available to reduce
the complexity of any environment, although the use of
defined categories may prematurely limit the search for new
information. These functional constraints can become
established as stable personality patterns. When these are
widely shared in a community they become 'cultural patterns'
and habitual solutions to social issues. They then influence
forms of socialization and the transmission of highly valued
belief systems, and become goals for social behaviour, or are
embodied in social movements. Any group responds (positively
or negatively) to those individuals whose beliefs are inconsistent
with the 'normal' beliefs, and the accepted beliefs are validated
by social sanctions to define 'reality'. The problems that
remain include distinguishing commitment from a (superficial)

consensual assent or simple conformity, and identifying the ways in which new beliefs can gain acceptance.

In any social situation it is necessary to evaluate, judge and interpret information to know what is happening. This is especially the case when social groups are in interaction or in conflict. An individual's interpretation of what is being transacted will reflect his previously learned rules, or those habitual conclusions that use ready formulations like the 'class war', 'religious conflict' or 'capitalism'. These may be slogans to inhibit critical thinking and their use can preclude an evaluation of the characteristics or contingencies of a situation. They can also provide a language to facilitate communication. So ideologies force conclusions that are self-validating, and they control and restrict the behaviour of individuals and groups. But their positive role as sets of beliefs, ideas and ideals that form a person's development and identity should not be underestimated.

References

Abelson, R. P. (1968), 'Simulation of social behaviour', in
G. Lindzey and E. Aronson (eds.), *Handbook of Social Psychology*,
vol. 2, ch. 12, Addison-Wesley.

Abelson, R. P. *et al.* (1968), *Theories of Cognitive Consistency:
A Sourcebook*, Rand McNally.

Adorno, T. W., Frenkel-Brunswick, E., Levinson, D. J., and
Sanford, R. N. (1950), *The Authoritarian Personality*, Harper &
Row.

Allen, R. O., and Spilka, B. (1967), 'Committed and consensual
religion: a specification of religious prejudice relationships',
J. for Scientific Study of Religion, vol. 6, pp. 191–206.

Allport, G. W. (1935), 'Attitudes', in C. M. Murchison (ed.),
Handbook of Social Psychology, Clark University Press.

Allport, G. W. (1937), *Personality: a Psychological Interpretation*,
Constable.

Allport, G. W. (1942), 'The use of personal documents in
psychological science', *soc. Sci. Res. Council Bull.*, no. 49.

Allport, G. W. (1954), 'The historical background of modern social
psychology', in G. Lindzey (ed.), *Handbook of Social Psychology*,
ch. 7, Addison-Wesley.

Allport, G. W. (1966), 'Traits revisited', *Amer. Psychol.*, vol. 21,
pp. 1–10.

Allport, G. W., Vernon, P. E., and Lindzey, G. (1960), *Manual for
the Study of Values*, 3rd edn, Houghton Mifflin.

Almond, G. A. (1954), *The Appeals of Communism*, Princeton
University Press.

Apter, D. E. (1964), *Ideology and Discontent*, Free Press.

Argyle, M. (1969), *Social Interaction*, Methuen.

Argyle, M., and Little, B. R. (1972), 'Do personality traits apply to
social behaviour?', *J. Theory soc. Behav.*, vol. 2, pp. 1–35.

Arien, A. (1967), 'The role of ideology in determining behaviour', *sociol. Rev.*, vol. 15, pp. 47–57.

Aronson, E., and Carlsmith, J. M. (1968), 'Experimentation in social psychology', in G. Lindzey and E. Aronson (eds.), *Handbook of Social Psychology*, vol. 2, ch. 9, Addison Wesley.

Aronson, E., and Mills, J. (1959), 'The effect of severity of initiation on liking for a group', *J. abnorm. soc. Psychol.*, vol. 59, pp. 177–81.

Asch, S. E. (1952), *Social Psychology*, Prentice-Hall.

Atkinson, J. W., and Feather, N. T. (1966), *A Theory of Achievement Motivation*, Wiley.

Bakan, D. (1965), 'Some thoughts on reading Augustine's Confessions', *J. for Scientific Study of Religion*, vol. 5, pp. 149–52.

Bannister, D., and Mair, J. M. M. (1968), *The Evaluation of Personal Constructs*, Academic Press.

Bay, C. (1970), 'Political and apolitical students: facts in search of theory', in E. E. Sampson, H. A. Karn, *et al.*, *Student Activism and Protest*, Jossey-Bass.

Becker, H. S. *et al.* (1961), *Boys in White: Student Culture in Medical School*, University of Chicago Press.

Bem, D. J. (1970), *Beliefs, Attitudes and Human Affairs*, Brooks/Cole.

Berkowitz, L. J., and Lutterman, K. G. (1968), 'The traditional socially responsible personality', *Pub. Opin. Q.*, vol. 32, pp. 169–87.

Bettelheim, B., and Janowitz, M. (1950/1964), *Social Change and Prejudice*, Free Press.

Blishen, B. R. (1969), *Doctors and Doctrines: the Ideology of Medical Care in Canada*, University of Toronto Press.

Bogardus, E. S. (1925), 'Measuring social distances', *J. appl. Sociol.*, vol. 9, pp. 299–308.

Borgatta, E. F., and Evans, R. R. (eds.) (1968), *Smoking, Health and Behaviour*, Aldine.

Borgatta, E. F., and Lambert, W. W. (eds.) (1968), *Handbook of Personality Theory and Research*, Rand McNally.

Bormuth, John R. (1970), *On the Theory of Achievement Test Items*, University of Chicago Press.

Brazziel, W. F. (1969), 'A letter from the South', *Harvard educ. Rev.*, vol. 39, pp. 348–56.

Brock, T. C. (1962), 'Implications of conversion and magnitude of cognitive dissonance', *J. for Scientific Study of Religion*, vol. 1, pp. 198–203.

Bronfenbrenner, V. (1958), 'Socialization and social class through time and space', in E. E. Maccoby, T. M. Newcomb, and E. L. Hartley (eds.), *Readings in Social Psychology*, pp. 400–425, Holt, Rinehart & Winston.

Brown, B. O. (1968), 'An empirical study of ideology in formation', *Rev. Rel. Res.*, vol. 9, pp. 79–87.

Brown, L. B. (1962a), 'Religious belief in two student societies', *Australian J. Psychol.*, vol. 14, pp. 202–209.

Brown, L. B. (1962b), 'A study of religious belief', *Brit. J. of Psychol.*, vol. 55, pp. 259–72.

Brown, L. B. (1964), 'Classifications of religious orientation', *J. for Scientific Study of Religion*, vol. 4, pp. 91–9.

Brown, L. B. (1965), 'Aggression and denominational membership', *Brit. J. soc. clin. Psychol.*, vol. 4, pp. 175–8.

Brown, L. B. (1966), 'The structure of religious belief', *J. for Scientific Study of Religion*, vol. 5, pp. 259–72.

Brown, L. B. (1969), *Confirmation and Religious Belief*, University of Wellington Publications in Psychology, no. 22.

Brown, R. (1965), *Social Psychology*, Free Press.

Brown, R. (1970), *Psycholinguistics: Selected Papers*, Free Press.

Brown, R., and Lenneberg, E. H. (1954), 'A study in language and cognition', *J. abnorm. soc. Psychol.*, vol. 49, pp. 454–62.

Bruner, J. S., and Goodman, C. C. (1947), 'Value and need as organizing factors in perception', *J. abnorm. soc. Psychol.*, vol. 47, pp. 33–44.

Bruner, J. S., and Postman, L. (1948), 'Symbolic value as an organizing factor in perception, *J. soc. Psychol.*, vol. 27, pp. 203–208.

Buhler, C. (1971), 'Basic theoretical concepts of humanistic psychology', *Amer. Psychol.*, vol. 26, pp. 378–86.

Burnham, J. C. (1968), 'Historical background for the study of personality', in E. F. Borgatta and W. W. Lambert (eds.), *Handbook of Personality Theory and Research*, ch. 1, Rand McNally.

Butler, D. E., and Stokes, D. (1969), *Political Change in Britain: Forces Shaping Electoral Choice*, Macmillan.

Campbell, A. *et al.* (1960), *The American Voter*, Wiley.

Campbell, D. T. (1967), 'Stereotypes and the perception of group differences', *Amer. Psychol.*, vol. 22, pp. 817–29.

Campbell, D. T., and Fiske, D. W. (1959), 'Convergent and discriminant validation by the multitrait – multimethod matrix', *Psychol. Bull.*, vol. 56, pp. 81–105.

Cantril, H. (1941), *The Psychology of Social Movements*, revised edn, 1963, Wiley.

Cartwright, D., and Zander, A. (1968), *Group Dynamics: Research and Theory*, 3rd edn, Harper & Row.

Cawte, J. E. (1964), 'A psychiatric service in the North', *Australian J. soc. Issues*, pp. 20–32.

Charters, W. W., and Newcomb, T. M. (1958), 'Some attitudinal effects of experimentally increased salience of a membership group', in E. E. Maccoby, T. M. Newcomb, and E. L. Hartley (eds.), *Readings in Social Psychology*, Holt, Rinehart & Winston, pp. 276–81.

Child, I. L. (1954), 'Socialization', in G. Lindzey, and E. Aronson (eds.), *Handbook of Social Psychology*, Addison-Wesley.

Chin, R., and Chin, A. (1969), *Psychological Research in Communist China, 1949–1966*, MIT.

Christie, R. (1956a), 'Eysenck's treatment of the personality of Communists', *Psychol. Bull.*, vol. 53, pp. 411–30.

Christie, R. (1956b), 'Some abuses of psychology', *Psychol. Bull.*, vol. 53, pp. 439–51.

Christie, R., and Geis, F. (1968), 'Some consequences of taking Machiavelli seriously', in E. F. Borgatta and W. W. Lambert (eds.), *Handbook of Personality Theory and Research*, ch. 18, Rand McNally.

Christie, R., and Geis, F. L. (1970), *Studies in Machiavellianism*, Academic Press.

Christie, R., and Jahoda, M. (1954), *Studies in the Scope and Method of the Authoritarian Personality*, Free Press.

Cockburn, A., and Blackburn, R. (1969), *Student Power*, Penguin.

Cohen, J., and Struening, E. (1962), 'Attitudes to the mentally ill in the psychiatric personnel of two large mental hospitals', *J. abnorm. soc. Psychol.*, vol. 64, pp. 349–60.

Comrey, A. L. (1966), 'Comparison of personality and attitude variables', *educ. psychol. Measurement*, vol. 26, pp. 853–60.

Conrad, H. S. (1967), 'Clearance of questionnaires with respect to "invasion of privacy", public sensitivities, ethical standards, etc.', *Amer. Psychol.*, vol. 22, pp. 356–9.

Coombs, C. H. (1964), *Theory of Data*, Wiley.

Coulthard, M. (1969), 'Discussion of restricted and elaborated codes', *educ. Rev.*, vol. 22, pp. 38–50.

Cumming, E., and Cumming, J. (1957), *Closed Ranks*, Harvard University Press.

Danziger, K. (1958), 'Value differences among South African students', *J. abnorm. soc. Psychol.*, vol. 57, pp. 339–46.

Davies, A. F. (1966), *Private Politics*, Melbourne University Press.

Dawson, J. M. L. (1969), 'Attitude change and conflict among Australian aborigines', *Australian J. Psychol.*, vol. 21, pp. 101–16.

Deconchy, J. P. (1968), 'Sujets feminins et sujets masculins dans un groupe a finalité religieuse', *Archives de Sociologie des Religions*, vol. 26, pp. 97–110.

Denzin, N. K. (1971), 'The work of little children', *New Society*, 7 January, pp. 12–14.

Dittes, J., and Kelley, H. H. (1956), 'Effects of different conditions of acceptance upon conformity to group norms', *J. abnorm. soc. Psychol.*, vol. 53, pp. 629–36.

Dittes, J. E. (1969), 'Psychology of religion', in G. Lindzey and E. Aronson (eds.), *Handbook of Social Psychology*, vol. 5, ch. 44, Addison-Wesley.

Dittes, J. E. (1971), 'Two issues in measuring religion', in M. P. Strommen (ed.), *Research on Religious Development*, Hawthorn.

Dixon, N. F. (1971), *Subliminal Perception: the Nature of a Controversy*, McGraw-Hill.

Dreeben, R. (1967), 'Contributions of schooling to the learning of norms', *Harvard educ. Rev.*, vol. 37, pp. 219–37.

Edelson, M. (1971), *The Idea of a Mental Illness*, Yale University Press.

Edwards, A. L. (1957), *Techniques of Attitude Scale Construction*, Appleton-Century-Crofts.

Ehrlich, C. (1971), 'The male sociologists' burden: the place of women in marriage and family texts', *J. Marriage and the Family*, vol. 33, pp. 421–30.

Elkind, D. (1963), 'The child's conception of his religious denomination: III. The Protestant child', *J. gen. Psychol.*, vol. 103, pp. 291–304.

Endler, N. S., Hunt, J. McV., and Rosenstein, A. J. (1962), 'An *S-R* inventory of anxiousness', *psychol. Monograph*, vol. 76, no. 536.

Erikson, E. H. (1950), *Childhood and Society*, Penguin, revised edn, 1965.

Erikson, E. H. (1959), *Young Man Luther: a Study in Psychoanalysis and History*, Faber.

Erikson, E. H. (1970), *Gandhi's Truth on the Origins of Militant Non-Violence*, Faber.

Etzkowitz, H. (1971), 'The male sister: sexual separation of labor in society', *J. Marriage and the Family*, vol. 33, pp. 431–4.

Eysenck, H. J. (1953), *Uses and Abuses of Psychology*, Penguin.

Eysenck, H. J. (1954), *The Psychology of Politics*, Routledge & Kegan Paul.

Eysenck, H. J. (1956a), 'The psychology of politics and the personality similarities between fascists and communists', *Psychol. Bull.*, vol. 53, pp. 431–8.

Eysenck, H. J. (1956b), 'The psychology of politics: a reply', *Psychol. Bull.*, vol. 53, pp. 177–82.

Eysenck, H. J. (1965), *Smoking, Health and Personality*, Basic Books.

Eysenck, H. J. (1971), 'Social attitudes and social class', *Brit. J. soc. clin. Psychol.*, vol. 10, pp. 201–212.

Eysenck, H. J. (1972), *Psychology is About People*, Allen Lane.

Feather, N. T. (1964), 'Acceptance and rejection of arguments in relation to attitude strength, critical ability and intolerance of inconsistency', *J. abnorm. soc. Psychol.*, vol. 69, pp. 127–36.

Feldman, S. (ed.) (1966), *Cognitive Consistency: Motivational Antecedents and Behavioral Consequents*, Academic Press.

Feldman, K. A., and Newcomb, T. (1969), *The Impact of College on Students*, Jossey-Bass.

Ferguson, L. W. (1939), 'Primary social attitudes', *J. Psychol.*, vol. 8, pp. 217–23.

Festinger, L. (1950), 'Experiments in group belongingness', in J. Miller (ed.), *Experiments in Social Process*, McGraw-Hill.

Festinger, L., Riecken, H. W., and Schachter, S. (1956), *When Prophecy Fails*, Harper & Row.

Fichter, J. H. (1953), 'The marginal Catholic: an institutional approach', *soc. Forces*, vol. 32, pp. 167–73.

Fishbein, M. (1967), *Readings in Attitude Theory and Measurement*, Wiley.

Fishbein, M., and Raven, B. H. (1962), 'The *AB* Scales: an operational definition of belief and attitude', *human Rel.*, vol. 15, pp. 35–44.

Flacks, R. (1967), 'The liberated generation: an exploration of the roots of student protest', *J. soc. Issues*, vol. 23, pp. 52–75.

Flavell, J. H. (1968), *The Development of Role-Taking and Communication Skills in Children*, Wiley.

Fransella, F., and Bannister, D. (1967), 'A validation of repertory grid technique as a measure of political construing', *Acta Psychologica*, vol. 26, pp. 97–106.

Freeman, H. E., and Giovannoni, J. M. (1969), 'Social psychology of mental health', in G. Lindzey, and E. Aronson (eds.), *Handbook of Social Psychology*, vol. 5, ch. 45, Addison-Wesley.

Freedman, J. L., and Sears, D. O. (1965), 'Selective exposure', in *Advances in Experimental soc. Psychol.*, vol. 2, pp. 57–97.

Frenkel-Brunswick, E. (1954), 'Further explorations by a contributor to the authoritarian personality', in R. Christie and M. Jahoda, *Studies in the Scope and Method of the Authoritarian Personality*, Free Press.

Freud, S. (1910), *Leonardo*, Penguin, revised edn., 1963.

Gamson, W. A., and Modigliani, A. (1966), 'Knowledge and foreign policy opinions: some models for consideration', *Pub. Opin. Q.*, vol. 30, pp. 187–99.

Gibson, G. (1972), 'Chinese medical practice and the thoughts of Chairman Mao', *soc. Sci. and Medicine*, vol. 6, pp. 67–93.

Gilbert, D. C., and Levinson, D. J. (1956), 'Ideology, personality and institutional policy in the mental hospital', *J. abnorm. soc. Psychol.*, vol. 53, pp. 263–71.

Gillespie, J. M., and Allport, G. W. (1955), *Youth's Outlook on the Future: a Cross-National Study*, Doubleday.

Glock, C. Y., and Stark, R. (1965), *Religion and Society in Tension*, Rand McNally.

Godin, A. (1964), 'Belonging to a Church: what does it mean psychologically?', *J. for Scientific Study of Religion*, vol. 3, pp. 204–215.

Gorsuch, R. (1968), 'The conceptualization of God as seen in adjective ratings', *J. for Scientific Study of Religion*, vol. 7, pp. 56–64.

Goslin, D. A. (ed.) (1969), *Handbook of Socialization Theory and Research*, Rand McNally.

Graebner, O. E. (1964), 'Child concepts of God', *rel. Educ.*, vol. 69, pp. 234–41.

Graham, L. R. (1972), *Science and Philosophy in the Soviet Union*, Knopf.

Green, B. F. (1964), 'Attitude measurement', in G. Lindzey, *Handbook of Social Psychology*, ch. 9, Addison-Wesley.

Green, R. T., and Stacey, B. G. (1964), 'Was Torquemada tenderminded?', *Acta Psychologica*, vol. 22, pp. 250–71.

Greer, G. (1971), *The Female Eunuch*, Paladin.

Gross, M. (1962), *The Brain Watchers*, Random House.

Grouch, C. (1970), *The Student Revolt*, Bodley Head.

Gurin, P. *et al.* (1969), 'Internal–external control in the motivational dynamics of negro youth', *J. soc. Issues*, vol. 25, pp. 29–53.

Gusfield, J. R. (1970), *Protest, Reform and Revolt: a Reader in Social Movements*, Wiley.

Guttman, L. (1944), 'A basis for scaling qualitative data', *Amer. sociol. Rev.*, vol. 9, pp. 139–50.

Harris, N. (1971), *Beliefs in Society: the Problem of Ideology*, Penguin.

Harvey, O. J. (1970), 'Conceptual systems and attitude change', in P. Warr (ed.), *Thought and Personality*, Penguin.

Havighurst, R. J., and Keating, B. (1971), 'The religion of youth', in M. P. Strommen (ed.), *Research on Religious Development*, Hawthorn.

Heider, F. (1958), *The Psychology of Interpersonal Relations*, Wiley.

Herbst, P. G. (1954), 'Conceptual framework for studying the family', in O. A. Oeser, and S. B. Hammond (eds.), *Social Structure and Personality in a City*, Routledge & Kegan Paul.

Hess, R. D., and Shipman, V. C. (1965), 'Early experience and the socialization of cognitive modes in children', *Child. Devel.*, vol. 36, pp. 869–86.

Hess, R. D., and Torney, J. V. (1967), *The Development of Political Attitudes in Children*, Aldine.

Himmelweit, H. T., and Swift, B. (1969), 'A model for the understanding of school as a socializing agent', in P. Mussen *et al.*, *Trends and Issues in Developmental Psychology*, Holt, Rinehart & Winston.

Himmelweit, H. T., and Swift, B. (1971), *Adolescent and Adult Authoritarianism Re-examined*, unpublished manuscript.

Hollander, E. P., and Willis, R. H. (1967), 'Some current issues in the psychology of conformity and non-conformity', *Psychol. Bull.*, vol. 68, pp. 62–76.

Hovland, C. J., Harvey, O. J., and Sherif, M. (1957), 'Assimilation and contrast in reactions to communication and attitude change', *J. abnorm. soc. Psychol.*, vol. 55, pp. 244–52.

Hudson, L. (1970a), 'The choice of Hercules', *Bull. of the Brit. psychol. Soc.*, vol. 23, pp. 287–92.

Hudson, L. (1970b), *Frames of Mind*, Penguin.

Hyde, K. E. (1965), *Religious Learning in Adolescence*, Oliver & Boyd.

Ingleby, D. (1970), 'Ideology and the human sciences', *The Human Context*, vol. 2, pp. 159–90.

Inkeles, A. (1955), 'Social change and social character: the role of parental mediation', *J. soc. Issues*, vol. 11, pp. 12–23.

Inkeles, A., and Levinson, D. J. (1969), 'National character: the study of modal personality and sociocultural systems', in G. Lindzey and E. Aronson (eds.), *Handbook of Social Psychology*, vol. 4, ch. 34, Addison-Wesley.

James, W. (1907), *Pragmatism: a New Name for Some Old Ways of Thinking*, Longman.

Jaunzems, I., and Brown, L. B. (1972), 'A social psychological study of Latvian immigrants in Canberra', *Int. Migration*, vol. 10, pp. 53–70.

Jekels, L. (1952), 'The turning point in the life of Napoleon I', in *Selected Papers*, Imago.

Jensen, A. R. (1969), 'How much can we boost IQ, and scholastic achievement?', *Harvard educ. Rev.*, vol. 39, pp. 1–123.

Jones, E. E., and Gerard, H. B. (1967), *Foundations of Social Psychology*, Wiley.

Jones, H. G. (1971), 'In search of an idiographic psychology', *Bull. Brit. psychol. Soc.*, vol. 24, pp. 279–90.

Jones, M. (1970), 'They want it now', *New Statesman*, 30 October, p. 561.

Kagan, J., and Moss, H. A. (1962), *From Birth to Maturity: the Fels Study of Psychological Development*, Wiley.

Kagitcibasi, C. (1970), 'Social norms and authoritarianism: a Turkish–American comparison', *J. Person. soc. Psychol.*, vol. 16, pp. 444–51.

Katz, D. (1957), 'The two-step flow of communication: an up-to-date report on the hypothesis', *Pub. Opin. Q.*, vol. 21, pp. 61–78.

Katz, D. (1960), 'The functional approach to the study of attitudes', *Pub. Opin. Q.*, vol. 24, pp. 163–204.

Katz, D. (1965), 'Nationalism and strategies of international conflict resolution', in H. C. Kelman (ed.), *International Behaviour: a Social-Psychological Analysis*, Holt, Rinehart & Winston.

Katz, D., and Stotland, E. (1969), 'A preliminary statement to a theory of attitude structure and change', in S. Koch (ed.), *Psychology: a Study of a Science*, McGraw-Hill.

Kelley, H. H., and Stabelski, A. J. (1970), 'Social interaction of cooperators' and competitors' beliefs about others', *J. Person. soc. Psychol.*, vol. 16, pp. 66–91.

Kelman, H. C. (ed.) (1965), *International Behaviour: a Social-Psychological Analysis*, Holt, Rinehart & Winston.

Keniston, K. (1960), *The Uncommitted: Alienated Youth in American Society*, Harcourt Brace & World.

Keniston, K. (1968), *Young Radicals*, Harcourt, Brace & World.

Kiesler, C. A. (1971), *The Psychology of Commitment: Experiments Linking Behaviour to Belief*, Academic Press.

Kiesler, C. A., Collins, B. E., and Miller, N. (1969), *Attitude Change: a Critical Analysis of Theoretical Approaches*, Wiley.

Kimmel, P. (1969), 'Research on work and the worker in the United States', in J. P. Robinson, R. Athanasiou and K. B. Head, *Measures of Occupational Attitudes and Occupational Characteristics*, Survey Research Center, pp. 17–24.

Kirscht, J. P., and Dillehay, R. C. (1967), *Dimensions of Authoritarianism: a Review of Research and Theory*, University of Kentucky.

Klapp, O. E. (1968), *Symbolic Leaders: Public Drama and Public Men*, Minerva.

Klausner, S. Z. (1964), 'The religio-psychiatric movement: changing ideology of the movement', *Rev. of Religious Res.*, vol. 6, pp. 7–22.

Klineberg, O. (1954), *Social Psychology*, Holt, Rinehart & Winston.

Kluckhohn, F. R., and Strodtbeck, F. L. (1961), *Variations in Value Orientation*, Harper & Row.

Kohlberg, L. (1969), 'Stage and sequence: the cognitive-developmental approach to socialization', in D. A. Goslin (ed.), *Handbook of Socialization Theory and Research*, Rand McNally.

Korten, D. C. (1962), 'Situational determinants of leadership structure', *J. conflict Res.*, vol. 6, pp. 222–35.

Kotre, J. (1971), *The View from the Border: a Social-Psychological Study of Current Catholicism*, Gill & Macmillan.

Krech, D., and Crutchfield, R. S. (1948), *Theory and Problems of Social Psychology*, McGraw-Hill.

Laing, R. D. (1967), *The Politics of Experience*, Penguin.

Lane, R. E. (1962), *Political Ideology: Why the American Common Man Believes What he Does*, Free Press.

Lanternari, V. (1963), *The Religions of the Oppressed: a Study of Modern Messianic Cults*, MacGibbon & Kee.

La Pierre, R. T. (1934), 'Attitudes *v.* actions', *soc. Forces*, vol. 13, pp. 230–37.

Lasswell, H. D. (1930), *Psychopathology and Politics*, revised edn, 1960, Viking Press.

Lenski, G. (1963), *The Religious Factor*, Doubleday.

Levinson, D. J. (1954), 'The inter-group relations workshop: its psychological aims and effects', *J. Psychol.*, vol. 38, pp. 103–26.

Levinson, D. J. (1957), 'Authoritarian personality and foreign policy', *J. conflict Res.*, vol. 1, pp. 37–47.

Levinson, D. J., and Huffman, P. E. (1955), 'Traditional family ideology and its relation to personality', *J. Person.*, vol. 23, pp. 251–73.

Levinson, D. J., and Sanford, N. (1944), 'A scale for the measurement of anti-Semitism', *J. of Psychol.*, vol. 17, pp. 339–70.

Lieberman, S. (1956), 'The effects of changes in roles on the attitudes of role occupants', *human Rel.*, vol. 9, pp. 385–402.

Lifton, R. J. (1961), *Thought Reform and the Psychology of Totalism*, Norton.

Likert, R. (1932), 'The method of constructing an attitude scale', *Archives of Psychol.*, no. 140, pp. 44–53.

Lindner, R. (1953), 'Political creed and character', *Psychoanalysis*, vol. 2, pp. 10–33.

Lindzey, G. (ed.) (1954), *Handbook of Social Psychology*, Addison-Wesley.

Lindzey, G., and Aronson, E. (eds.) (1968), *Handbook of Social Psychology*, 2nd edn, Addison-Wesley.

Lipman-Blumen, J. (1972), 'How ideology shapes women's lives', *Scient. Amer.*, vol. 22, pp. 34–42.

Lovibond, S. (1967), 'The effect of media stressing crime and violence upon children's attitudes', *soc. Prob.*, vol. 15, pp. 91–100.

Lutzker, D. R. (1960), 'Internationalism as a predictor of cooperative behaviour', *J. conflict Res.*, vol. 4, pp. 426–30.

McClelland, D. C. (1958), 'The use of measures of human motivation in the study of society', in J. W. Atkinson (ed.), *Motives in Fantasy, Action and Society*, Van Nostrand.

McClelland, D. C. (1961), *The Achieving Society*, Van Nostrand.

McClintock, C. G. *et al.* (1963), 'Internationalism–isolationism, strategy of the other player and two-person game behaviour', *J. abnorm. soc. Psychol.*, vol. 67, pp. 631–5.

McClintock, C. G., and Turner, H. A. (1962), 'The impact of college upon political knowledge, participation and values', *human Rel.*, vol. 15, pp. 163–76.

McClosky, H. (1958), 'Conscience and personality', *Amer. pol. sci. Rev.*, vol. 52, pp. 27–45.

McClosky, H., and Schaar, J. H. (1965), 'Psychological dimensions of anomie', *Amer. sociol. Rev.*, vol. 30, pp. 14–40.

McGregor, D. (1960), *The Human Side of Enterprise*, McGraw-Hill.

McGuigan, G. F. (1968), *Student Protest*, Methuen.

McGuire, W. J. (1968), 'Personality and susceptibility to social influence', in E. F. Borgatta and W. W. Lambert (eds.), *Handbook of Personality Theory and Research*, Rand McNally.

McGuire, W. J. (1969), 'The nature of attitudes and attitude change', in G. Lindzey and E. Aronson (eds.), *Handbook of Social Psychology*, Addison-Wesley.

Malcolm, X. (1966), *The Autobiography of Malcolm X*, Grove Press, Penguin edn, 1968.

Mannheim, K. (1936), *Ideology and Utopia*, Routledge & Kegan Paul.

Marlowe, D., and Gergan, K. J. (1969), 'Personality and social interaction', in G. Lindzey and E. Aronson (eds.), *Handbook of Social Psychology*, vol. 3, ch. 25, Addison-Wesley.

Marvick, D. (ed.) (1961), *Political Decision-Makers*, Free Press.

Marx, G. T. (1972), 'Perspectives on violence', *contemp. Psychol.*, vol. 17, pp. 128–31.

Marx, G. T., and Useem, M. (1971), 'Majority involvement in minority movements: civil rights, abolition and untouchability', *J. soc. Issues*, vol. 27, pp. 81–104.

Maslow, A. H. (1954), *Motivation and Personality*, Harper & Row.

Mauss, A. L. (1971), 'On being strangled by the stars and stripes', *J. soc. Issues*, vol. 27, pp. 183–202.

Maxwell, G. (1971), *Investigation into Attitudes Towards Issues Raised by Radical Youth Movements*, unpublished manuscript.

Merton, R. K. (1968), *Social Theory and Social Structure*, Free Press.

Middlebrook, P. N. (1972), 'The radical activist as "superpsyche"', *contemp. Psychol.*, vol. 17, pp. 19–20.

Milgram, S., and Toch, H. (1969), 'Collective behaviour: crowds and social movements', in G. Lindzey and E. Aronson (eds.), *Handbook of Social Psychology*, vol. 4, ch. 35, Addison-Wesley.

Miller, G. A. (1969), 'Psychology as a means of promoting human welfare', *Amer. Psychol.*, vol. 24, pp. 1063–75.

Miller, G. A., Galanter, E., and Pribram, K. H. (1960), *Plans and the Structure of Behaviour*, Holt, Rinehart & Winston.

Money-Kyrle, R. E. (1951), *Psychoanalysis and Politics: a Contribution to the Psychology of Politics and Morals*, Duckworth.

Moore, H. T. (1925), 'Innate factors in radicalism and conservatism', *J. abnorm. soc. Psychol.*, vol. 20, pp. 234–244.

Morlan, G. K. (1950), 'An experiment on the recall of religious material', *Religion in Life*, vol. 19, pp. 589–94.

Morris, C., and Jones, L. V. (1955), 'Value scales and dimensions', *J. abnorm. soc. Psychol.*, vol. 51, pp. 523–35.

Mortenson, U. (1972), 'Psychology in contemporary Germany', *New Zealand Psychol.*, vol. 1, pp. 34–9.

Murray, H. A. (1938), *Explorations in Personality*, Wiley, revised edn, 1962.

Murvar, V. (1971), 'Messianism in Russia: religious and revolutionary', *J. for Scientific Study of Religion*, vol. 10, pp. 277–338.

Neal, A., and Seeman, M. (1964), 'Organization and powerlessness: a test of the mediation hypothesis', *Amer. sociol. Rev.*, vol. 29, pp. 216–25.

Newcomb, T. M. (1943), *Personality and Social Change*, Dryden Press.

Newcomb, T. M. (1961), *The Acquaintance Process*, Holt, Rinehart & Winston.

Newcomb, T. M. *et al.* (1967), *Persistence and Change: Bennington College and its Students after Twenty-Five Years*, Wiley.

Oeser, O. A., and Emery, F. E. (1954), *Social Structure and Personality in a Rural Community*, Routledge & Kegan Paul.

O'Neil, W. M., and Levinson, D. J. (1954), 'A factorial exploration of authoritarianism and some of its ideological concomitants', *J. Person.*, vol. 22, pp. 449–63.

Osgood, C. E. *et al.* (1957), *The Measurement of Meaning*, University of Illinois Press.

Paige, J. M. (1965), 'Letters from Jenny', in P. J. Stone *et al.* (eds.), *The General Inquirer*, MIT.

Parkin, F. (1968), *Middle-Class Radicalism: the Social Bases of the British Campaign for Nuclear Disarmament*, Manchester University Press.

Parsons, T., and Shils, E. A. (eds.) (1951), *Toward a General Theory of Action*, Harvard University Press.

Peabody, D. (1966), 'Authoritarianism scales and response bias', *Psychol. Bull.*, vol. 65, pp. 11–23.

Piaget, J. (1933), 'Children's philosophies', in C. Murchison (ed.), *A Handbook of Child Psychology*, 2nd edn, Clark University Press.

Piaget, J. (1947), *The Psychology of Intelligence*, Routledge & Kegan Paul, revised edn, 1950.

Pruyser, P. (1968), *Dynamic Psychology of Religion*, Harper & Row.

Radzinowicz, L. (1966), *Ideology and Crime*, Heinemann.

Remmers, H. H. (1934), 'Generalized attitude scales', *J. soc. Psychol.*, vol. 5, pp. 298–312.

Richardson, A. (1957), 'The assimilation of British immigrants in Australia', *human Rel.*, vol. 10, pp. 157–66.

Riegel, K. F. (1972), 'Influence of economic and political ideologies on the development of developmental psychology', *Psychol. Bull.*, vol. 78, pp. 129–41.

Riesman, D. (1952), *Faces in the Crowd*, Yale University Press.

Robinson, J. P., Athanasiou, R., and Head, K. B. (1969), *Measures of Occupational Attitudes and Occupational Characteristics*, Survey Research Center.

Robinson, J. P., Rusk, J. G., and Head, K. B. (1968), *Measures of Political Attitudes*, Survey Research Center.

Robinson, J. P., and Shaver, P. R. (1969), *Measures of Social Psychological Attitudes*, Survey Research Center.

Rokeach, M. (1960), *The Open and Closed Mind*, Basic Books.

Rokeach, M. (1964), *The Three Christs of Ypsilanti*, Knopf.

Rokeach, M. (1967), 'Authoritarianism scales and response bias: comment on Peabody's paper', *Psychol. Bull.*, vol. 67, pp. 349–55.

Rokeach, M. (1969), 'An experimental analysis of the organization of belief systems', in *Beliefs, Attitudes and Values*, Jossey-Bass.

Rokeach, M. (1970), 'A value analysis of the disputed Federist papers', *J. Person. soc. Psychol.*, vol. 16, pp. 245–50.

Rokeach, M., and Hanley, C. (1956), 'Eysenck's tender-mindedness dimension: a critique', *Psychol. Bull.*, vol. 53, pp. 169–76.

Rose, A. M. (1962), 'Alienation and participation: a comparison of group leaders and the "Mass"', *Amer. sociol. Rev.*, vol. 27, pp. 834–8.

Rosenberg, M. J., and Gardner, C. W. (1958), 'Case report: some dynamic aspects of post-hypnotic compliance', *J. abnorm. soc. Psychol.*, vol. 57, pp. 351–66.

Rosenberg, M. J. (1960), *Attitude Organization and Change*, Yale University Press.

Rosenberg, M. J. (1965), 'Images in relation to the policy process: American public opinion on cold-war issues', in H. C. Kelman (ed.), *International Behaviour: a Social-Psychological Analysis*, Holt, Rinehart & Winston.

Rosenblatt, P. C. (1964), 'Origins and effects of group ethnocentrism and nationalism', *conflict Res.*, vol. 8, pp. 131–46.

Rothlisberger, F. J., and Dickson, W. J. (1939), *Management and the Worker*, Harvard University Press.

Rotter, J. B. (1966), 'Generalized expectancies for internal *v.* external control of reinforcement', *psychol. Monograph*, vol. 80, pp. 1–28.

Rudolph, L. I., and Rudolph, S. H. (1967), *The Modernity of Tradition: Political Development in India*, University of Chicago Press.

Russell, B. (1969), *The Autobiography of Bertrand Russell*, vol. 3, Allen & Unwin.

Sangster, P. (1963), *Pity my Simplicity: the Evangelical Revival and the Religious Education of Children, 1738–1800*, Epworth.

Sarbin, T. R., and Allen, V. L. (1969), 'Role theory', in G. Lindzey and E. Aronson (eds.), *Handbook of Social Psychology*, vol. 1, ch. 7, Addison-Wesley.

Sarbin, T. R., Taft, R., and Bailey, D. E. (1960), *Clinical Inference and Cognitive Theory*, Holt, Rinehart & Winston.

Sargent, W. (1958), *Battle for the Mind: the Mechanics of Indoctrination, Brain Washing and Thought Control*, Penguin, revised edn, 1961.

Scanzoni, J. (1968), 'System analysis of dissolved and existing marriages', *J. Marriage and the Family*, vol. 30, pp. 452–6.

Schachter, S. (1965), 'A cognitive-physiological view of emotion', in O. Klineberg, and R. Christie (eds.), *Perspectives in Social Psychology*, Holt, Rinehart & Winston.

Schmidl, F. (1962), 'Psychoanalysis and history', *psychoanalytic Q.*, vol. 31, pp. 532–48.

Scott, W. A. (1959), 'Empirical assessment of values and ideologies', *Amer. sociol. Rev.*, vol. 24, pp. 299–310.

Scott, W. A. (1962), 'Cognitive complexity and cognitive flexibility', *Sociometry*, vol. 25, pp. 405–14.

Scott, W. A. (1965), 'Psychological and social correlates of international images', in H. C. Kelman (ed.), *International Behaviour: a Social-Psychological Analysis*, Holt, Rinehart & Winston.

Scott, W. A. (1968), 'Attitude measurement', in G. Lindzey and E. Aronson (eds.), *Handbook of Social Psychology*, vol. 2, ch. 11, Addison-Wesley.

Scott, W. A. (1969), 'Structure of natural cognitions', *J. of Person. and Soc. Psychol.*, vol. 12, pp. 261–78.

Sears, D. O. (1969), 'Political behaviour', in G. Lindzey and E. Aronson (eds.), *Handbook of Social Psychology*, vol. 5, ch. 41, Addison-Wesley.

Sears, R. R., Maccoby, E. E., and Levin, I. F. (1957), *Patterns of Child Rearing*, Harper & Row.

Shaw, M. E., and Wright, J. M. (1967), *Scales for the Measurement of Attitudes*, McGraw-Hill.

Sheatsley, P. B. (1966), 'White attitudes towards the Negro', *Daedalus*, vol. 95, pp. 217–38.

Sherif, M., and Sherif, C. W. (1969), *Social Psychology*, Harper & Row.

Sherif, C. W., Sherif, M., and Nebergall, R. E. (1965), *Attitude and Attitude Change: the Social Judgement – Involvement Approach*, Saunders.

Skinner, B. F. (1972), *Beyond Freedom and Dignity*, Cape.

Smith, M. B., Bruner, J. J., and White, R. W. (1956), *Opinions and Personality*, Wiley, revised edn, 1964.

Snider, J. G., and Osgood, C. E. (1969), *Semantic Differential Technique: a Source Book*, Aldine.

Srole, L. (1956), 'Social integration and certain corollaries', *Amer. Sociol. Rev.*, vol. 21, pp. 709–16.

Stacey, B. G., and Green, R. T. (1968), 'The psychological bases of political allegiance among white-collar males', *Brit. J. soc. clin. Psychol.*, vol. 7, pp. 45–60.

Stachowiek, J. G., and Moss, C. S. (1965), 'Hypnotic alteration of social attitudes', *J. of Person. and Soc. Psychol.*, vol. 2, pp. 73–83.

Stone, P. J. *et al.* (eds.) (1966), *The General Inquirer*, MIT.

Storr, A. (1969), 'The man', in A. J. P. Taylor (ed.), *Churchill: Four Faces and the Man*, Allen Lane.

Strachey, L. (1921), *Eminent Victorians*, Chatto & Windus.

Straus, M. A. (1969), *Family Measurement Techniques – Abstracts of Published Instruments, 1935–1965*, University of Minnesota Press.

Strauss, A. *et al.* (1964), *Psychiatric Ideologies and Institutions*, Free Press.

Swanson, G. F. (1960), *The Birth of the Gods: the Origin of Primitive Beliefs*, University of Michigan Press.

Taft, R. (1965), *From Stranger to Citizen*, University of Western Australia Press.

Tawney, R. H. (1926), *Religion and the Rise of Capitalism*, John Murray.

Thistlethwaite, D. (1950), 'Attitude and structure as factors in the distortion of reasoning', *J. abnorm. soc. Psychol.*, vol. 45, pp. 442–58.

Thomas, A., and Sillen, S. (1972), *Racism and Psychiatry*, Brunner/Mazel.

Thouless, R. H. (1935), 'The tendency to certainty in religious belief', *Brit. J. Psychol.*, vol. 26, pp. 16–31.

Thurstone, L. L. (1928), 'Attitudes can be measured', *Amer. J. Sociol.*, vol. 33, pp. 529–54.

Toch, H. (1966), *Psychology of Social Movements*, Methuen.

Tomkins, S. (1963), 'Left and right: a basic dimension of ideology and personality', in R. W. White (ed.), *The Study of Lives*, Atherton.

Triandis, H. C., and Triandis, L. M. (1962), 'A cross-cultural study of social distance', *psychol. Monograph*, vol. 76.

Turner, R. H. (1966), 'Acceptance of irregular mobility in Britain and the United States', *Sociometry*, vol. 29, pp. 334–52.

Turner, A. N., and Lawrence, P. R. (1965), *Industrial Jobs and the Worker: an Investigation of Response to Task Attributes*, Harvard Graduate School of Business Administration.

Tyson, A. (1971), 'Homage to Catatonia', *New York, Review of Books*, 11 February.

Vacchiano, R. B., Strauss, P. S., and Hochman, L. (1969), 'The open and closed mind: a review of dogmatism', *Psychol. Bull.*, vol. 71, pp. 261–73.

Vernon, G. M. (1968), 'The religious "nones": a neglected category', *J. for Scientific Study of Religion*, vol. 7, pp. 219–29.

Vernon, P. E. (1969), *Intelligence and Cultural Environment*, Methuen.

Warr, P. B., and Knapper, C. (1968), *The Perception of People and Events*, Wiley.

Warr, P. B., Schroeder, H. M., and Blackman, S. (1969), 'The structure of political judgement', *Brit. J. soc. clin. Psychol.*, vol. 8, pp. 32–43.

Warren, N. (1966), 'Social class and construct system: an examination of the cognitive structure of two social class groups', *Brit. J. soc. clin. Psychol.*, vol. 5, pp. 254–60.

Waterman, A. S., and Waterman, C. K. (1971), 'A longitudinal study of changes in ego identity status during the freshman year at College', *develop. Psychol.*, vol. 5, pp. 167–73.

Waxman, C. (ed.) (1969), *The End of Ideology Debate*, Simon & Schuster.

Webb, E. J. *et al.* (1966), *Unobtrusive Measures: Nonreactive Research in the Social Sciences*, Rand McNally.

Weiss, R. F. (1963), 'Defection from social movements and subsequent recruitment to new movements', *Sociometry*, vol. 26, pp. 1–20.

Weisz, A. E., and Taylor, R. L. (1969), 'American presidential assassination', *Diseases of the Nervous System*, vol. 30, pp. 659–68.

Weschler, I. R. (1950), 'An investigation of attitude toward labor and management by means of the error-choice method', *J. soc. Psychol.*, vol. 32, pp. 51–62.

Whiting, J. W., and Child, I. L. (1953), *Child Training and Personality*, Yale University Press.

Whyte, W. H. (1956), *The Organization Man*, Simon & Schuster.

Wiberg, J. L., and Blom, G. E. (1970), 'A cross-national study of attitude content in reading primers', *Int. J. Psychol.*, vol. 5, pp. 109–22.

Wilson, G. D. (1970), 'Is there a general factor in social attitudes? Evidence from a factor analysis of the conservatism scale', *Brit. J. soc. clin. Psychol.*, vol. 9, pp. 101–7.

Wilson, G. D., and Patterson, J. R. (1968), 'A new measure of conservatism', *Brit. J. soc. clin. Psychol.*, vol. 7, pp. 264–9.

Wolfenstein, M. (1951), 'The emergence of fun morality', *J. of Soc. Issues*, vol. 7, pp. 15–25.

Wolfinger, R. E. *et al.* (1964), 'America's radical right: politics and ideology', in D. Apter (ed.), *Ideology and Discontent*, Free Press.

Woodmansee, J. J. (1970), 'The pupil response as a measure of social attitudes', in G. F. Summers (ed.), *Attitude Measurement*, Rand McNally.

Woolcott, P. (1966), 'Some considerations of creativity and religious experience in St Augustine of Hippo', *J. for Scientific Study of Religion*, vol. 5, pp. 273–83.

Wright, D. S. (1971), *The Psychology of Moral Behaviour*, Penguin.

Wrightsman, L. S. (1972), 'Wallace supporters and adherence to "law and order"', in L. Bickman, and T. Henchy, *Beyond the Laboratory*, McGraw-Hill.

Zajonc, R. B. (1960), 'The process of cognitive tuning in communication', *J. abnorm. soc. Psychol.*, vol. 61, pp. 159–67.

Zajonc, R. B. (1968), 'Attitudinal effects of more exposure', *J. Person. soc. Psychol.*, vol. 9, pp. 1–27.

Zilboorg, G. (1941), *A History of Medical Psychology*, Norton.

Zigler, E., and Child, I. L. (1969), 'Socialization', in G. Lindzey, and E. Aronson (eds.), *Handbook of Social Psychology*, vol. 3, ch. 24, Addison-Wesley.

Index